Finding Our Way through the Wilderness

A Journey for Lent or Other Days of Spiritual Reflection and Prayer

John Michael Helms

Erica Cooper

Published in the United States by FaithLab, Macon GA.
www.thefaithlab.com

ISBN 978-0-9839863-2-4

What Others Say

Like muscles, our spiritual awareness needs to be stretched if we are to become strong and spiritually mature. This is a book that will stretch you spiritually. Michael Helms and Erica Cooper are not only gifted writers, they also see spiritual realities in the whole sweep of human experience. Spend a few minutes each day with this book, and it will make such a difference in your life that you will return to it regularly.

R. Alan Culpepper
Dean, McAfee School of Theology
Mercer University

Written so plainly that a child will understand, yet laced with the kind of depth and history that scholars will embrace. What an extraordinary achievement that is!

Ronda Rich
Best-selling author of *What Southern Women Know About Faith*

The simple straightforward stories of the Lenten journeys are spellbinding and captivating. The prayers are refreshing and penetrating and the total journey is a delight. I cannot wait to use it as a guide at Lent or even on my next spiritual retreat. Wow, what a great read and adventure! This is a great addition to my own journey.

Ken Smith
President
Ken Smith Ministries

Michael Helms and Erica Cooper have written a book that will inspire many. Their uplifting messages, stories, and prayers are powerful and revealing. While reading *Finding Our Way Through the Wilderness*, I felt calm coming into my chaotic life. I highly recommend this book to any and all.

Jean Sasson
New York Times and international bestselling author of:
Princess: A True Story of Life Behind the Veil in Saudi Arabia
Growing up Bin Laden: Osama's Wife and Son Share
        their Secret Life

If ever the world were a wilderness, it would be today. Economic and social unrest have created a maze with confusing twists and turns. More than a GPS to guide us, we need a sense of spiritual direction and the confidence to find our way, with His help. In Michael Helms and Erica Cooper's *Finding Our Way Through the Wilderness*, the safe route is clearly defined. Just as our GPS speaks to us, their masterful storytelling offers a calming assurance that we can navigate through the wilderness. I didn't read it once. I read it twice. And I'll read it again. It's that good.

Dink NeSmith
President
Community Newspapers, Inc.

Also by
John Michael Helms

Finding Our Way: An Introspective Journey
Through the Labyrinth of Life

Hoping Liberia:
Stories of Civil War from
Africa's First Republic

Finding Our Way with the Magi:
A Daily Guide Through the Season of Advent

Dedicated to Caroline Slawson
Her Spiritual Journey
Through the Wilderness
Has Been an Inspiration to Many

For H.W.

Acknowledgments

This book was years in the making. No one writes apart from their past or their present. Sometimes a book shows evidence of that more than others, and this is one of those.

I brought the idea of this book and part of this manuscript with me to Jefferson, Georgia. Since many of these pages had their genesis in my weekly discipline of writing for *The Moultrie Observer*, I must acknowledge editor Dwain Walden for the opportunity to write for that paper. The weekly discipline of writing for the general public did more for my writing career than any one thing.

The public can be very kind and very blunt in their comments about a printed piece. I've been given accolades and I've been called names. There were some days I wasn't so sure I had much to thank Dwain for because I was as likely to be fodder for the "rant and rave" section of the paper as anyone. In the "rant and rave" section, people can call or write anonymously and comment on almost anything. Sometimes the "almost anything" was my article.

If you write for the public, you better be ready to take some hits, and I took a few. So, along with my improved writing skills, I developed a thicker skin, but never so thick that criticism didn't sting at least a little.

What hurts worse than criticism is to see a printed piece with a glaring error. It's like waking up in the morning with a huge zit right in the middle of your forehead on a day when you are having your picture taken. What can you do? That's why you need another set of eyes on what you write before it's printed. My friend Andrea Savage proofed my material for *The Moultrie Observer* and was the first 'proofer' for this book. She's been very helpful in keeping me from embarrassing myself. She's also made me a better technical writer, but I'd probably still have a problem getting an A in her English class: too many revisions.

In Jefferson I've met a very humble English professor who has been the final sieve for some of my projects. Dr. Diana Young teaches college and is another excellent consultant who has helped with this project. She has gone the extra mile to ensure our work meets publishing standards. As if these women weren't enough, our colleague in ministry, Richard Dickson, gave the manuscript one last read. God has blessed Erica and me with these people to help ensure that the manuscript is as clean as possible.

My present place of ministry also shapes the pages of this book. I pastor First Baptist Church, Jefferson, Georgia. As a pastor, my life turns around the lives of these people. I share their joys, celebrations, and successes in life. I also carry their burdens, grief, doubts, pain, and problems, and try to help them transform what's not healthy into what is healthy. I try to help them focus life away from themselves (denying self as Jesus described it) and onto the worship of God and to the service of others. They in turn do the same for me. In fact, their loving service to others is one of the things that attracted me to this church.

As a part of this community, they sometimes carry me. They assist me in my journey. They minister to me. I feel their love and concern for my family. I sense we are on a journey together. I hope you get that feeling from reading this book; we are all on a journey together as the experiences of life bond us all together. The wilderness touches us all. Hopefully, you are a part of a family of believers that will journey with you during wilderness times in your life.

I am delighted that you are reading this book. While there is value in writing for myself, there's more value in knowing that what I write might help other people on their spiritual journey.

One person who has helped me on my spiritual journey is Erica Cooper. She joined the staff of First Baptist Church of Jefferson in 2010 as our Associate Pastor/Minister to Families. Erica is an excellent administrator, pastoral care giver and preacher. She has a gifted presence with families, helping them shape their lives around the love and person of Jesus Christ and deal with the issues that arise in their daily lives. Children and parents love Erica. Her joy bubbles over onto each, and they catch the love of Jesus from her before she teaches it to them.

One of her greatest skills is listening. Because she listens well and observes what's going on in the lives of families and the world around her, her prayers take on a life that ministers to people deep down where the pain is, where springs of joy originate, where questions lurk, where fear resides, where guilt haunts, where happiness exudes, or where depression is tucked and hidden from others. She helps us confess our sins and understand how grace comes from God. You can tell that she's not only heard about the wilderness, but she's experienced it. Because of that and because of the presence of the Holy Spirit in her life, she says what most of us think from time to time but are not able to put into words.

For these reasons and others, I invited Erica Cooper to write the prayers for this book. They could stand alone. However, as a companion to the daily readings, you have something to ponder and a focused prayer to give you direction as you find your way through the wilderness and through the season of Lent.

If you are reading this book during a time other than the Lenten season, you will find that it's just as valuable because wilderness experiences do not calendar themselves. They come when they come. A book like this can be one tool that gives you the encouragement to keep moving or in some cases to be still, to keep praying, to keep ministering, to keep exploring the scriptures, to keep hoping, to keep listening for God's voice, to keep struggling, to keep questioning and seeking, and to keep allowing God to help you find your way.

John Michael Helms
Jefferson, Georgia

The opportunity to write the prayers for this book came to me as a surprise and a blessing. I am honored to be a part of this project and to work alongside one of my favorite people, Michael Helms.

I would like to thank my family who has given me wonderful support in all of my ministry endeavors, especially my father, Bud Hartman, who never fails to engage me in some theological or ecclesiastical discussion when we get together. My mother Becky has always been a cheerleader for my vocation, still making every effort to come and hear me preach. My parents have been dedicated lay leaders in their home church of First Presbyterian ever since we moved to the college town of Athens, Georgia. Growing up I could ask for no better example of putting one's faith into action, as they have spent their entire lives serving the church and their community.

My sister Tanya and her husband Paul have given me the wonderful gift of being a godmother to their son Max, who was born in April 2010. Since becoming an aunt and a godmother, I have become more aware of God's magnificence, mystery and sense of humor revealed in humanity. This child grows and changes by the second, and it has been astonishing to watch him transform into a funny, precocious, and precious little boy. I look forward to discovering God's amazing adventures through Max.

My husband Chris has given me wonderful support. He is the smartest and most humble person I have ever met. I am fortunate to have him as my best friend. He is the one who gives me space when I need to write, or entertains me when I need a good distraction. He listens to me when I am frustrated. He laughs at my stupid jokes. He assures me that I am good at what I do when I am in doubt. He tells me to get to work when I am being lazy. No one could ask for a better partner in life.

I am very appreciative of my church, First Baptist of Jefferson. This church has welcomed Chris and me with open arms...and great food! The believers who make up First Baptist challenge me each day to become a better Christian. I have never been surrounded by such a mission-minded group of folks, who make themselves living sacrifices to make our community a better place. I am so fortunate to worship and serve alongside them.

And finally, I would not have my name on this book if it were not for the invitation from Michael Helms. Few people get to work with someone who is a true servant leader. I learn something new from Michael every day I work with him. You will never meet someone more dedicated to his work, whether that work is preaching, writing, leading, care-giving, or entertaining children by riding a unicycle in the sanctuary. Michael puts his full heart into everything he does, and that is what makes him a true "renaissance" pastor.

From the first day I met Michael, I noticed that he takes a true interest in others. He wants to learn more about other people; he wants to know their stories. Michael places great value in others' stories, in others' celebrations or tragedies, in others' hopes or fears. Michael remembers these stories in his heart and validates these stories by re-telling them in his writing. I believe others grow closer to God through listening to Michael's stories. So if you have a story to tell, be sure to tell it to Michael.

Erica Cooper
Jefferson, Georgia

Table of Contents

Explaining Lent—
A Season of
Spiritual Preparation

Introduction

The first signs of spring are beginning to emerge during the season of Lent. Pollen from trees like the ash, pine, oak, hickory and pecan; grasses like ragweed, ryegrass, and lemongrass; common flowers like the honeysuckle, sunflower, poppy and clover—all add to the release of a light yellow tinge that soon covers everything from our cars to our porches.

Robins are beginning to arrive. It will not be long before hummingbirds will make their long migration back to my part of the world in North Georgia. Soon farmers will be turning the soil and preparing the ground for seed. Butterflies will begin to emerge from their chrysalises. Bream will begin to spawn in ponds and riverbeds. All around us nature is waking up. The roses and azaleas around town will begin to put forth new flowers. The bluebirds will begin building new nests in the boxes erected for them in various places. Preparation is being made for another cycle of growth.

Within this cycle of growth we call spring, Easter is not far away. It finds its way onto the spring calendar every year, its date moving around like a Mexican jumping bean. Perhaps you've wondered why the date for Easter jumps around each year. Christmas is a fixed date, so why not Easter?

In the early church, bishops in the East and those in Rome were celebrating the Easter feast on different Sundays. There was no unanimity on the date of Jesus' resurrection. Thus, when the bishops came together to address some deep theological matters in Nicaea in 325 A.D., they addressed this practical issue of ensuring that the same day was chosen to celebrate the Easter feast every year. Since there was no strong consensus on the original date, they felt that a Sunday was the most appropriate day of the week to celebrate it. They decided if they changed to a uniform date there would be no future arguments about the true Easter date.[1] The new system they developed was determined by the phases of the moon.

Tying the dates to the moon phases ensured that no one could get the dates wrong again. However, because the moon phases differ from month to month, this ensured that the Easter feasts would jump around within a small window of dates. Such dating sounds strange to modern ears, but it made very good sense to people of the fourth century who were tied to the land and the heavens. The Council of Nicaea decided that Easter would be celebrated on the Sunday following the first full moon that occurred after the spring equinox. Because of the way the lunar calendar cycles, Easter must occur between March 22 and April 25. Thus, in some years Easter comes much earlier in the spring than in others (Wikipedia).

The season that prepares us for Easter is known as Lent. The word Lent is derived from the Old English lencten, which means "lengthen."[2] "Originally, in the early church, Lent spanned 40 weekdays, beginning on Ash Wednesday, moving through Holy Week's Maundy Thursday and Good Friday, and concluding the Saturday before Easter. Lent became a time of preparation for those who were to be baptized, a time of concentrated study and prayer before their baptism at the Easter Vigil. Those who had become believers during the year were baptized early Easter Sunday morning. As these new members were received into a living community of faith, the entire community was called to preparation. This also became a time when those who had been separated from the Church would prepare to rejoin the community."[3] "Today, Lent is marked by a time of prayer and preparation to celebrate Easter. Since Sundays celebrate the resurrection of Jesus, the six Sundays that occur during Lent are not counted as part of the 40 days of Lent, and are referred to as the Sundays in Lent" (Bratcher).

"The number 40 is connected with many biblical events, but especially with the 40 days Jesus spent in the wilderness preparing for His ministry and overcoming temptations that could have led Him to abandon His mission and calling. Christians today use this period for introspection, self-examination, and repentance" (Bratcher).

This book is written with these purposes in mind. While you might read the book from the comfort of your favorite chair, in the sunshine on the patio of your home, on the go as you move quickly traveling in a new area of work, or while you are away for a time of rest, it is designed to challenge you, give you hope, help you focus your mind on Christ through prayer, and to help you find your way through a life that can seem like a wilderness of confusion, grief, temptation, heartache, trouble, despair, and confusion.

Preparations are being made all around us for another growth cycle. Why should that be any different within our spiritual lives? Spiritual growth is more intentional than not. Jesus modeled that spiritual growth involves spiritual disciplines.

That's the reason His trip into the wilderness is so intriguing. The Bible says that He was led there by the Holy Spirit. Led there! We typically try to avoid a wilderness, but the Holy Spirit led Jesus to one. There He battled temptation. There He solidified His calling and established the kind of ministry He would have.

Easter is on the calendar every year. Easter will come and go whether we do any planning or not. However, Easter will not produce much spiritual growth in us without preparation. We may find ourselves stooping down to peer inside the empty tomb on Easter morning without a great deal of excitement or awe unless we prepare ourselves for that morning and for the words of the angel: "He is not here; he has risen, just as he said. Come and see the place where he lay" (Matthew 28:6)[4].

This journey begins on Ash Wednesday, or it can begin any time you feel led to walk into the wilderness to focus on spiritual disciplines so you can hear the voice of God.

Ash Wednesday is a day when we remember our mortality, our finiteness. It is a day that we are reminded that our time on this earth is brief. The Psalmist says, "Men and women don't live very long; like wildflowers they spring up and blossom, but a storm snuffs them out just as quickly, leaving nothing to show they were here" (Psalm 103:15-16, The Message).

Without such reminders, our eyes become fixed on the glitz and glitter of the world, on things that pass away. We chase after fool's gold and mirages out in a wilderness until we realize that we are lost and thirsty, having stuffed our pockets full of worthless shiny rocks.

This book is designed to help us empty our pockets of the fool's gold and pick up pieces of the cross. It's designed to help us find our way out of the wilderness and into the world where we can find our place of service.

This book can serve as fertilizer for the seeds of faith that may be planted this time of the year. The strength of the words within these covers really depends on the willingness you have to enter into a struggle with God in your own wilderness, to pray the prayers and make them your own, and to arrive at Easter with a renewed spirit.

If a farmer misses the window to plant a crop, he will not have time to reap a harvest. If we waste precious days or precious years, we can't get them back. However, Lent reminds us to seize the moment. There's grace available right now! Make the season of Lent an intentional season of growth. Make Lent a spiritual journey toward the cross, and then you'll bend down and be in awe of the empty tomb. Easter will be a day of celebration and not just another day!

Who Will Remember You?

Lent 1

Ash Wednesday

The Egyptian Pharaohs were concerned with their immortality. To insure safe passage into the afterlife, they built huge pyramids, which housed their mummified bodies at death. When death came, these mummies were buried in tombs along with food, valuable jewels, and immaculately designed masks and ornamentation, which they thought would assist them in the afterlife.

Modern man has considered such efforts to achieve passage from one life to the next the misguided hopes of an ancient civilization. However, the Pharaohs' quest for immortality has not been abandoned. Our methods are simply more sophisticated. For many people in the modern world, the quest for immortality has little to do with living again in another world.

The primary twenty-first century way to immortality is to make sure our heroes and sometimes our villains are never forgotten. People of fame have become the Pharaohs of our society: sports stars, millionaires, those with political clout, national heroes, and movie celebrities, to name a few.

Will the Beatles ever be forgotten? Won't all future generations see the film clips of Jesse Owens demoralizing Adolf Hitler and his idea of a superior race during the 1936 Olympics? Will the world ever forget the likes of John F. Kennedy or movie stars like Marilyn Monroe and Elvis? Is there an American who has not seen footage of Neil Armstrong taking the first steps on the moon? These people will never be forgotten, nor should they be. For many, this is the meaning of immortality, to never be forgotten.

Some of us may be fortunate enough to have fifteen minutes of fame, a phrase coined by artist Andy Warhol. But only a small number will be remembered forever. Thus, for many, lasting memory among the masses has become the ticket to immortality.

To have one's life and accomplishments recorded through the lens of a camera, to have one's life catalogued in a hall of fame, or to have one's work displayed in a museum—these are the pyramids of the twenty-first century.

Even those who espouse evil can achieve a twisted celebrity status that spans generations. Hasn't the name "Jesse James" survived more than a century? Won't people forever remember John Wilkes Booth and Lee Harvey Oswald? The promise to never be forgotten seemed to drive the insanity of Timothy McVeigh. Some people are driven by the thought of living forever in infamy.

Like the ancient Egyptians, we believe that as long as a few make it to immortal status, albeit an earthly one, then life will have been worth living. Like the workers who built the great pyramids, we are developing a culture that seeks to make some people into gods.

We pay our homage to them and help feed the false belief that what matters is that centuries from now people will be talking about some of us.

Only a few of us will be remembered in books or in film, have buildings named after us, or be known for some great heroic deed or discovery. As important as such contributions may be to modern society, none of this changes the fact that the grave awaits us all. In the end, the grave is the great equalizer. The grave is a chilling reminder that regardless of how much one is adored, appreciated, loved, or even worshiped, death comes to everyone.

When death comes, what will be of ultimate importance isn't whether we are remembered by people, but that the Creator of the universe remembers us. Will our name be written in the Lamb's Book of Life? For if it is not, we die not only once, but twice. This is the vision the Apostle John saw and wrote about in the Book of The Revelation: "The lake of fire is the second death. If anyone's name was not found written in the book of life, he was thrown into the lake of fire" (Revelation 20:14-15).

A man dying on a cross on a hill in Jerusalem two thousand years ago found the key to eternal living just hours before he died. Turning to a holy man who was being crucified beside him, he said, "'Jesus, remember me when you come into your kingdom.' Jesus answered him, 'I tell you the truth, today you will be with me in paradise'" (Luke 23:42-43).

It's not likely that we will accomplish anything in life that will cause our names to be remembered beyond a generation or two. But that kind of immortality shouldn't be of concern to us anyway. What should be important to us is whether Jesus remembers us and allows us to be present with Him in paradise.

So the pondering of our mortality is important because we must face the fact that beyond this life we will either live forever with Christ or we will be forever separated from Christ. It's highly unlikely that we will live forever with Christ if we have never pondered our mortality. For if we never think about dying, then how can we ever think about living eternally with Christ?

To put it another way, a sure way to find ourselves in the worst kind of wilderness is to never ponder the thought of one. Being separated from Christ is the worst kind of wilderness a person can ever be in. If a person is separated from Christ at death, that wilderness experience will last for an eternity.

Today is Ash Wednesday. This is a day on which Christians ponder our mortality. We encourage all people to focus on words like these found in James: "What is your life? You are a mist that appears for a little while and then vanishes" (James 4:14).

When we take inventory of our lives, we can reevaluate our priorities. We can ask ourselves whether we are placing emphasis on the most important things. If not, we can make midcourse corrections. If little things are claiming the most important spots, we can make changes, lest we find ourselves wandering in a wilderness.

At an Ash Wednesday service, a minister takes some ashes, places them on a person's forehead, makes the sign of the cross and says something like, "Remember you are dust, and to dust you shall return. Turn away from sin and be faithful to Christ" (Genesis 3:19 and Mark 1:15).

Most people feel a little bit uncomfortable walking around with an ashy cross on their foreheads. It's a bit humbling actually. Those who experience this service in the morning go through the entire day, not just thinking about their ashy forehead, but about the deeper meaning, that they should repent of any sin that is present in their lives. It's also a reminder that sin is ultimately what causes death and makes all of us return to dust.

It is our sin that creates some wilderness experiences in our lives: dead places where joy, love, peace, and hope dry up and wither away. Through repentance we can put the wilderness in perspective. Through repentance, the wilderness can bloom and come to life.

During this first day of Lent, we prepare for God to come afresh in our lives. We prepare for God's victory over death in the Easter event, which gives us the great hope that we too will one day receive that same victory. On that day, death will once and for all be defeated, when the dead in Christ shall rise.

Until then, the sign of an ashy cross is a reminder that although death will come to us, we don't have to live in a wilderness of fear or despair. Death doesn't have the last word!

While we may be forgotten by future generations, it won't matter because we have the same promise given to the thief on the cross who asked Jesus to remember him. Just as Jesus promised that sinner a place with Him in paradise, Jesus extends that same promise to all who place their faith in Him.

Prayer

God of Life,

We are nothing but dust. We are soil. We are worm food. In Your over-whelming grace, You gave us life and instructed us to take care of the world and everything in it. We confess, Lord, that we waste Your gift and do not fulfill our calling. Instead, we use our time clinging to pride, feigning self-sufficiency, and worshiping celebrity.

On this day we stand at the edge of Your wilderness. You call us to leave behind the sins that have covered up our need for You. You call us to face the reality of death. You call us to journey through Your wild-ness, to learn and grow in Your ways, ways which don't make sense to this world. You call us to come before You as our true selves, ashamed and terrified of being forgotten.

As we wear these ashes today, may this death mark remind us of our need for You, God of Life. Without You we would have no breath. Without You we have no hope for life. Give us strength to take our first steps in this wilderness journey, though they seem difficult and strange. Guide us through this barren land of sin and shame toward Your glori-ous Garden of Life. Amen.

Strength to Stand
on the Stormy Banks
Lent 2

Seventy years ago, Hitler's Nazi regime was in full force. Among its goals was the elimination of those believed to be inferior to the Aryan race. Hitler wanted to control the world, which included the Christian church. The Christian church in America didn't feel the undercurrent, but the Christian church in Germany did.

Once in power Hitler brought the church under Nazi control by organizing the provinces of Lutheran churches under a single Reich bishop. Ludwig Muller, a fervent Nazi, was elected to head the church. He quickly placed two restrictions on the clergy: 1) a clergyman must be politically reliable and 2) the clergy must accept the superiority of the Aryan race.[5]

On January 4, 1934, Reich Bishop Muller issued a decree ordering pastors not to say anything in their sermons in opposition to the orders handed down to them. But on the same day he issued his decree, 320 elders and ministers went on record at Barmen in opposition to these restrictions. Clinging to the historical Confessions of Faith, this group of rebels against Hitler's regime called themselves the Confessing Church. Some paid dearly for their presence at that meeting by imprisonment or execution (Graves).

Oh, how we take our religious freedom for granted! Oh, how we take our church freedom for granted! The freedoms you and I enjoy today are not freedoms the church has enjoyed throughout its history, and they are not freedoms that people in many parts of the world enjoy today.

According to Christian Solidarity International, more Christians died for their faith in the twentieth century than at any other time in history. Gordon Conwell Theological Seminary reports an average of 171,000 Christians worldwide are martyred for their faith each year.[6]

Our country was established, in part, by people who sought relief from persecution because of their religion, making the dangerous journey to these shores to worship as they chose. However, as soon as colonies were established, these same people were setting up their own exclusionary religious rules.

It took a man named Roger Williams to cut a path of religious freedom in the new land. His action to establish a colony where people of any religious persuasion or even none at all could settle still has implications for religious freedom in America and continues to have theological implications for many Christians.

Unlike most settlers, Williams befriended the Native Americans and defended their property rights. As a man of faith, Williams had a deep desire to share with the Native Americans the gospel of Christ. He learned their language and their culture. While his relationship with the Indians grew stronger, his relationship with his own colony grew weaker. He was eventually banished from the English colony.

Why should we defend religious freedom? Take Jesus as an example. Jesus stepped into our world and into the Greek culture as a Jewish man with strong religious beliefs and claims about the kingdom of God. In the pages of the New Testament we read of several confrontations between Jesus and the established religious leaders of his day. He challenged their understanding of God. In return, they picked up stones to kill Him on more than one occasion.

We should have a passion to preserve religious freedom for others and ourselves because religious freedom was a right that Jesus claimed for Himself. Others tried to take it from Him, but they could not. You may be thinking, "Well, they killed Him, didn't they?" They killed Him, but they never took His religious freedom because He never gave it up.

When Pilate was trying to determine what to do with Jesus, he asked, "Where do you come from?" But Jesus did not answer. "'Do you refuse to speak to me?' Pilate said. 'Don't you realize I have power either to free you or to crucify you?' Jesus answered, 'You would have no power over me if it were not given to you from above'" (John 19:9-11).

While Jesus challenged the religious authorities, He never denied their right to believe differently than He did. He clearly laid out the consequences for their wrong understanding of God and practices of God's law, but He never sought to eliminate them, harm them, or do any kind of evil to them.

Though we enjoy religious freedom in America, a large percentage of the earth's population does not. Christians must be concerned about the suffering and oppression of people everywhere. We must fight for basic human rights and religious liberty for all people while we seek to share the love of Christ with a lost world.

While we take up such noble causes, we will continue to go through wilderness periods. As long as people are being oppressed, they need to be pointed to hope and salvation.

Through two millenniums, oppressed people have found hope in John's Revelation. The last book of the Bible was written during a time when the church was being persecuted. Revelation was written to a church that had gone underground in order to survive. Many Christians were arrested, beaten and killed because they professed to be disciples of Jesus.

As the Christian movement was in danger of being eliminated, hope came through the words of John the Apostle, who had been arrested and exiled to the island of Patmos. From that island, John could see across the Jordan River. I don't mean in a literal sense. I mean he could see a new day when God's people would no longer have to worry about the evil from without or the evil from within.

In the midst of persecution John could see a day when the trials and tribulations of this world would be over. John could see across the Jordan and what he saw was inviting: no more hunger, no more thirst, no more tears.

John could see a day when the rulers of the land would no longer oppress the people and when there would be no more underground churches, no more persecution of Christians, no more Third Reichs, no more genocides, no more war, no more injustice, no more prejudice, no more greed, and no more murder.

Our wilderness runs right up to the edge of the Jordan. We spend a lot of our lives wandering in the wilderness, trying to escape the wilderness, even at times denying that the wilderness is real. So it seems a little strange to have a time on the Christian calendar to ask Christians to actually seek the wilderness. Yet that, in part, is exactly what the season of Lent is about.

Part of Lent is about moving out of our comfort zone as we evaluate ourselves spiritually. When we go into the wilderness intentionally, it has far greater potential to teach rather than destroy.

Jesus sought the wilderness after His baptism and there He determined the course His ministry would take. For forty days He denied Himself the pleasure of food and He fought temptation. Because Jesus overcame all the temptation He ever faced in life, Hebrews proclaims that "we do not have a high priest who is unable to sympathize with our weaknesses, but we have one who has been tempted in every way, just as we are—yet was without sin. Let us then approach the throne of grace with confidence, so that we may receive mercy and find grace to help us in our time of need" (Hebrews 4:15-16).

Over these forty days of Lent, you are encouraged to intentionally enter the wilderness. Create your own kind of wilderness experience in the midst of your regular everyday activities. Carve out some time to be still, to ponder, to question, to listen, to fast, to give up something that will help you focus on Jesus. Make yourself uncomfortable enough that you are reminded that you are in the midst of a disciplined spiritual journey.

It could be that there's no need to create a wilderness experience. Life may have already done that for you. On this side of the Jordan, the banks are stormy, as Samuel Stennett wrote in a hymn first published in 1787.

How's the weather where you stand? I hope the sun is shining, but some of you may be standing on stormy banks. Others of you have been there already. The rest of us will be there one day.

We may not have the personal kind of pain the Lutheran church felt when the Nazis seized control, or the pain that the Apostle John felt as he wrote Revelation from the island of Patmos, but suffering is suffering. It just comes in varying degrees and at different times.

The stormier the banks of our lives become, the more the words of John's Revelation mean to us and the more we yearn for what's on the other side of the Jordan, not only for ourselves, but for people whose lives are lived without the basic freedoms and rights we enjoy.

As long as we travel this life, there will be stormy banks. The longer people stand on stormy banks, the greater will be our desire to sing about a Promised Land: a place where there is no more hunger, no more thirst, and no more weeping.

By God's grace, I am bound for that Promised Land, and I hope you are too. But in the meantime, we must move through the wilderness. While longing for what's on the other side of the Jordan, we need to continue to work to make things better here. Since we have a Savior who has already traveled through the wilderness on our behalf, we can move through our wildernesses with confidence, knowing that Jesus will provide us with mercy and grace in our times of need.

Prayer

God of Enduring Strength,

There are so many in our world facing the stormy banks of life. Today, we pray for those suffering.

We pray for the millions of Christians facing the storm of persecution and oppression in North Korea, Iran, Afghanistan, Saudi Arabia, Somalia, Maldives, Yemen, Iraq, Uzbekistan, Laos, Pakistan, Eritrea, Mauritania, Bhutan, Turkmenistan, China, Qatar, Vietnam, Egypt, Chechnya, Comoros, Algeria, North Nigeria, Azerbaijan, Libya, Omen, Burma, Kuwait, Brunei, Turkey, Morocco, India, Tajikistan, United Arab Emirates, North Sudan, Zanzibar Islands, Tunisia, Syria, Djibouti, Jordan, Cuba, Ethiopia, Palestinian Territory, Bahrain, Kyrgyzstan, Bangladesh, Indonesia, Sri Lanka, Malaysia, Israel, and all other corners of the earth. Lord, give them Your strength.

We pray for the millions who face the storm of poverty, for those who are hungry, homeless, indebted, out of work, uninsured or facing any financial crisis. Lord, give them Your strength.

We pray for the millions who face the storm of illness, for those who have cancer, heart disease, diabetes, malnutrition, physical injury, HIV/AIDS, obesity, infertility, mental illness, behavior disorders, addiction, birth defects, malaria, disability, or any other sickness or disease. Lord, give them Your strength.

We pray for the millions who face the storm of grief, for the widows, widowers, orphans, those who have lost children, those who have lost friends, the abused, the neglected, those living in the chaos of war and political unrest, the lonely, the divorced, or the bullied. Lord, give them Your strength.

We pray for the millions who face the storm of unspeakable pain, those who have yet to ask for Your love. For the hopeless, the faithless, the despairing, the enraged, the confused, the ashamed, or those who suffer in silence. Lord, give them Your strength.

Almighty God, in this wilderness of life show us a way through these stormy waters. Hold us with Your strength and guide us with the wisdom, encouragement, compassion, mercy, hope and peace of Christ. Amen.

Create a Shade Over Others with Your Prayers

Lent 3

I appreciate trees. They give without demanding in return. They provide an abundance of oxygen for us to breathe, filtering the air, which we pollute. Some trees sacrifice their bark for medicine; others give their sap to make rubber or syrup. Still others make the ultimate sacrifice so we can have shelter over our heads, furniture in our rooms, or warmth in the midst of the winter. Trees give us nourishment from fruit and nuts. I also appreciate trees for their beauty.

Evergreens maintain their beauty year round while deciduous trees allow us to watch their leaves change colors throughout the year. I especially like the hardwoods that bud beautifully in the spring and provide dazzling yellows, radiant reds, obstreperous oranges, and common browns in the fall. They partner with the wind to carry each leaf to a new resting place. Once released from the trees, the leaves' work isn't completely over. Soon they will become a part of the soil, enriching it, which ultimately helps the tree clothe itself again in the spring. This cycle of life never ends.

In the summer I especially appreciate trees for their shade. The leaves are green at just the right time. We don't need their shade through the winter. Through the hot days of summer, trees provide us with needed shade from the hot, blistering sun without expecting any words of thanks from us. We borrow their shade as if we owned it. But the tree is never upset. It humbly takes the brunt of the sun for us—the hotter the day, the lower its branches bend to the earth, as if it's praying.

If the tree were praying, what would it be saying to our Creator?

Perhaps it would ask the Creator for its shade not to go to waste. Perhaps it would ask for a shower of rain, not a downpour, so the water would sink deep down to its roots. Maybe it would ask the Creator to use it in a mighty way—to be wood for a ship or a house; or perhaps something simple like a child's toy or a piece of furniture.

If there is any tree that might have such an ability, it would be an old oak that stands on the old Stewart home place in Brooks County, Georgia. This tree was planted in 1891. As the years went by, it gave shade to the home of W. J. Stewart, who brought his eight children there after the death of his second wife.

Mr. Stewart was a very devout man who held devotionals in the quiet shade of the tree each morning. He prayed in a loud voice for each of his eight children, calling them by name, and asking God's blessings upon them and also upon the generations of his family yet to come. Because of his consistent, devout actions of prayer, the tree became known in the family as "The Prayer Tree."

Mary, one of his twenty-one grandchildren, believes his prayers for future generations were answered, evidenced by the emphasis in prayer she saw in her generation and even in the one after hers.

If that tree could reveal what it learned from Mr. Stewart, what words of wisdom do you think it might repeat? I think that oak would say that its shade should remind us of the grace of God. God's grace is like the branches that reach out to embrace humanity, casting shade over the righteous and unrighteous alike.

The Psalmist said it best: "The LORD watches over you—the LORD is your shade at your right hand; the sun will not harm you by day, nor the moon by night" (Psalm 121:5-6).

How often have you sat under the Lord's shade without giving Him thanks? How many times have you been shielded from the heat of the day because of the shade that comes from the right hand of the Lord? Mr. Stewart understood that the shade of that oak was a proper place to meet the Lord.

The season of Lent is a wonderful time to establish a favorite place where you can go and meet the Lord each day. We set appointments with others at specific times and specific places and look forward to keeping those appointments, so why not do the same with the Lord?

We don't have to be legalistic about it, but we do need to be intentional. This is part of what it means to have a relationship with our God. It's part of the goodness of Lent—to enter into the discipline of pulling away from people and activities to fellowship with God through prayer, scripture reading, and meditation.

Our prayers should include words of thanksgiving, realizing that we all sit under trees we did not plant. As we pray, we should think about those whose shade we have borrowed and perhaps taken for granted. There are people in our lives who have been there so often with their shade of trust and care that we have come to expect it, perhaps even taking it for granted. These are people who have given out of love for us. Now that they have come to your mind, sometime this week, why not thank them for their love?

Through prayer, we can focus on the more important aspects of our living. Through prayer, we can be empowered to action. When we are empowered to action, this causes a chain reaction in God's kingdom. There's a life cycle to prayer just as there is one in nature. When the leaves fall from the trees, they become a part of the soil, enriching it, ultimately helping the tree clothe itself again in the spring.

Prayer works that way, too. Its benefits continue to enhance God's kingdom. The prayers of one person enhance the lives of others who in turn grow in their faith. Their prayers then are heard by God and their lives have a greater effect on the lives of others.

Perhaps that's why Jesus compared the kingdom to a seed. For the kingdom of heaven is "like a mustard seed, which is the smallest seed you plant in the ground. Yet when planted, it grows and becomes the largest of all garden plants, with such big branches that the birds of the air can perch in its shade" (Mark 4:30-32).

A man was sold a house with a garden overgrown with weeds. It took the man a long time to cut down the weeds and prepare the soil for new seeds. Eventually, the seeds sprouted and the garden began to blossom again into a beautiful area that anyone would have been proud to show. The local minister dropped by one day for a visit and commented to the gardener that he and God had made the plot into a beautiful showcase. Not especially excited about giving God much credit, the gardener said, "Well, you should have dropped by when God had the garden by himself."[7]

During Lent, weeds need to be cleared, soil needs to be turned, and seeds need to be planted in our spiritual lives. If this isn't done, eventually what we have in our lives is a wilderness.

We might not give God much credit, but God is busy working, planting seeds all the time, both in nature and in the spiritual world. God is busy through our spiritual disciplines. During Lent, God seeks to work through us to plant seeds of hope, love, repentance, and renewal. The soil is tilled first in prayer.

Begin by thinking of those whose prayers you benefited from through your spiritual journey. Of course, in many cases, we will never know who has cast a shade of prayer over us. Nevertheless, acknowledge that you now sit under spiritual trees you did not plant. This will help catapult you into becoming a spiritual mentor for someone else. Shade others through Lent with your prayers. As you pray for others, may the Lord "[watch] over you; [may] the Lord [be] your shade at your right hand; [may] the sun...not harm you by day, nor the moon by night" (Psalm 121:5-6).

Prayer

Praise for Prayer

In the still moments of our day:
      waiting for the coffee to brew,
      driving into work,
      making the short walk to the mailbox.
      The moments we turn off our televisions,
      tuck our children into bed,
      close our own eyes at night,
Lord, You are waiting and listening.

In the chaos of our world,
      the violence of war and upheaval,
      our polluted and abused environment,
      the oppression and persecution of minorities,
      our own broken and bruised relationships,
Lord, You are calling and convicting.

In our thanksgiving and celebrations,
      weddings,
      births,
      adoptions,
      family reunions,
      parties with friends,
      promotions,
      good news,
Lord, You are laughing and singing.

In the times of pain and grief,
       in hospital waiting rooms,
       in funeral parlors,
       in police stations,
       in ambulances,
       in psychologists' offices,
Lord, You are healing and hope-giving.

We praise You, Loving God, that in all of our prayers,
       You listen.
       You offer wisdom.
       You show joy.
       You give peace.

May we grow ever more faithful in our daily conversations with You. Amen.

It Takes Initiative to Get Out of the Wilderness

Lent 4

I once asked my younger son to write his grandfather a thank-you note for going with us to watch him compete in a diving competition in Indianapolis and sharing the expenses with us. I didn't think Ryan would take the initiative to do so without my asking. He wrote, "Dear Daddy John, thanks for going to the dive meet with Dad and me. Dad can be really boring sometimes and he gets lost a lot."

That sounded a little passive aggressive to me, but at least he wrote the note. I have to admit, I used to have a disease common to many males: I thought it was a strike against my intelligence and manhood to stop and ask for directions. We saw more scenery that way, but we also wasted more gas and time. Once I finally repented and took the initiative to purchase a GPS device, I have wandered far less in the wilderness and have had a much better relationship with my wife on our travels.

I don't think I've ever been lost for very long or ever spent the night away from home wondering if I'd ever get back. I've never been driven from my home or had my home taken from me. I've never gone to bed hungry or ever been homeless. I've never known what it's like to really wander in a wilderness of hopelessness. I do know people who have been in these situations, though.

In 1995 I traveled to Liberia for the first time with Olu Menjay, a Liberian, who at that time was a student at Duke Divinity School. Southern Baptist Missionary, Rev. John Mark Carpenter, brought him to the United States, rescuing him from refugee status during the earlier years of the Liberian civil war. Our trip together was Olu's first trip back to his country since the war began.

On our trip Olu and I had a one-night layover in the Ivory Coast. A missionary picked us up at the airport and boarded us at the Baptist Compound in Abidjan. It was there that I first met Olu's brother, Hugo.

Hugo was also displaced by the war in Liberia and was a refugee in Ghana at the time. He had made his way from Ghana to Abidjan by walking and catching rides to see Olu for just a few hours. I watched as Olu opened his suitcase and began sharing his clothes with Hugo. He pulled off his belt and gave it to his brother. We shared food with him and a bottled drink from the refrigerator. I gave him some money.

These two brothers were separated by a war, but their hearts were still joined with love. One was fortunate enough to have made it to the States for an education with hope for a better life. The other was struggling for survival, begging daily for food, but hoping for a better life. I could tell even then that he had initiative. He had come hundreds of miles without food or money to see his brother in hopes of receiving a few items of clothing and a few American dollars.

About three years later, Hugo was able to immigrate to the States on a study visa. He attended and later graduated from college and was able to attain a green card because of his refugee status. He then became the manager of a clothing store in the Atlanta area.

Once, I visited Hugo in his suburban Atlanta home. I was struck with the juxtaposition of Hugo the refugee struggling for survival and Hugo the lower middle-class American.

Hugo and Olu had been in a wilderness like few in America could imagine. They understood the meaning of war, poverty, death, and suffering. They also knew the meaning of hope and initiative.

I realize we have an immigration problem in America. We must get our arms around our borders and stop illegal immigration. However, Hugo and Olu represent how immigration should be done and how beneficial it can be to both the individual and society when it's done right. Immigration saved these two young men from an early death and from a refugee status as their country was ripped apart by a fourteen-year civil war.

Dr. Olu Menjay later earned degrees from Duke Divinity School and the International Baptist Theological Seminary in Prague, Czechoslovakia. He returned to Liberia and became the principal of Ricks Institute, investing in the future of his country through the lives of children and teenagers. He is a real hero of mine, demonstrating that people still can put aside desires for an easier life to invest in a higher calling of service to others.

He and his brother are examples that the difference in those who succeed and fail is often the difference between those who have opportunity and those who don't. Given the right opportunity, there would be many more Hugos and Olus who would excel in this world. But there is also another key component. Many others are given opportunity to succeed but squander it. For some reason their initiative never rises to shake hands with their opportunity. Before we can achieve a crown of success, we must decide whether we are willing to pay the price with initiative.

Sometimes, the future looks hopeless, but like Hugo and Olu Menjay, we must never give up. We must decide how much we really want to sweat. How far do we really want to run and at what pace? If we are in the wilderness, how far are we willing to walk, even for the promise of a few clothes, a little money, and a chance to see family for just a few moments? How much will we dream and to what lengths are we willing to go to make those dreams come true? The answers to questions like these await us every day we live in a wilderness.

Yet initiative isn't worth a dime if we spend it all building a house on sand or if we focus on the things of this world rather than on what will last forever, like faith, hope, and love. There are plenty of people with initiative who are placing it in all the wrong places. The Bible says that faith, hope, and love will remain when all else is gone. Perhaps Jesus was referring to such things when He said we should store up for ourselves "treasures in heaven, where moth and rust do not destroy, and where thieves do not break in and steal" (Matthew 6:20).

If we take this kind of initiative each day, the words of the Psalmist will come true for each of us: "Surely goodness and love will follow me all the days of my life, and I will dwell in the house of the LORD forever" (Psalm 23:6). On that day we will be thankful that the Lord took the initiative to prepare such an eternal home for us and that we took the initiative to store up treasures that last forever.

Lent is a time of self-examination. It is a time to focus on our initiative as it relates to the Kingdom of God. While Lent is known for giving up things that are not good for us or things that may distract us from God, what if we looked at Lent as a time to take up those disciplines that are good for us? The Christian faith is much more than a faith of "dos" than a faith of "don'ts." Both require initiative. Without initiative, the wilderness around us will only claim more of us.

During this Season of Lent, may the Holy Spirit move us away from that which is causing us to be distant from God and move us toward actions that are Christlike in nature.

Prayer

Lord,

Sometimes we feel lost in this wilderness. It is dark, and we soon lose the path of hope. Let our hearts remember the stories of others who have fought their way through desolate wastelands. Let us remember those who have made it through to the other side to delight in Your presence. Keep our eyes on Your path alone, God. Bless us with the initiative to follow the ways of Christ. Motivate us to keep putting one foot in front of the other, despite our fears, our exhaustion, and our doubts. And help us to notice those who are struggling beside us in this wilderness, that we may support one another through the places that have become too treacherous to navigate alone. Amen.

Has Pleasure Become an American Idol?

Lent 5

One of the oldest searches known to humanity is the search for happiness. Perhaps the widest path cut in this search is the path of pleasure. One of those who espoused this path was Epicurus, a Greek who lived more than 2,300 years ago.

According to Epicurus, the purpose of life is the pursuit of personal happiness, and by happiness he does not simply mean well-being. He means that we should pursue pleasure itself, sensuous pleasure. Epicurus believed that we should not worry ourselves about the afterlife because he did not believe there is an afterlife. Since we are going around only once, we might as well grab all the gusto we can get. Sounds like a beer commercial, doesn't it?

In a letter to Menoeceus, Epicurus wrote: "We recognize pleasure as the first good innate in us, and from pleasure we begin every act of choice and avoidance, and to pleasure we return again, using the feeling as the standard by which we judge every good."[8]

Epicurus is dead. But his ideas about life are not. In fact, in the search for happiness, the path of pleasure is as wide as ever. People are still using pleasure as the standard to judge every good. People often measure the goodness of something by how it makes them feel.

Most Americans don't simply eat to survive and be healthy. We eat because we like how something tastes. The better the taste, the more we eat. We will even do without food if we don't like how it tastes because we know we can get something later that tastes better—something that brings more pleasure. Since food brings us pleasure and exercise often doesn't, obesity has become a major problem for Americans.

People do not have sex simply because it's one of the most intimate experiences God designed to be shared between a husband and a wife; people have sex because it brings pleasure.

According to Alice Frying in her book, *Seven Lies About Sex*, people who have sex outside of marriage usually believe one of three things: (1) if we are truly in love, sex is okay; (2) if I want it so badly, it must be natural, and therefore, okay; (3) if God doesn't take away my desire, it must be okay. Following these as value statements means that the pursuit of pleasure is more important than the pursuit of holiness.[9]

C.S. Lewis said, "It is the stealing of the apple that is bad, not the sweetness. The sweetness is still a beam from the glory. That does not palliate the stealing. It makes it worse. There is sacrilege in the theft. We have abused a holy thing."[10]

We abuse a holy thing when sex is only about pleasure and people are only objects in our pursuit of fulfilling a desire.

Barna Research Group Online reports that in 2001 the most common basis for moral decision-making was doing whatever feels right or doing what is comfortable within a given situation. Nearly four out of ten teens (38%) and three out of ten adults (31%) described this as their primary consideration in decision-making. This is evidence that the philosophy of Epicurus is alive and well among us. Only 15% of those surveyed said their decisions came from values learned from their parents, and only 13% said their values came from the Bible.[11]

Here lies the source of many of our problems. As citizens, we have been taught that the pursuit of happiness is the right of every American. However, many of us are turning the pursuit of happiness into a god and often that god is the god of pleasure.

Dancing around it and bowing down to it make us feel good, and the more we feel good the more we want to dance. We are compelled to keep dancing because we are never completely satisfied. As soon as we sit down, the pleasure is gone, so we will dance until we fall down in exhaustion and frustration.

A strange plant grows in the jungle called the strangler fig. It is a quick-growing plant much like the kudzu vine in our part of the country. As the plant goes up the tree, its roots wind themselves around the tree trunk, stealing nourishment that the tree needs.[12]

The plant grows bigger and bigger until it has completely encased the tree. The large leaves of the plant keep necessary light from the tree. The tree is shielded from the light of the sun, and eventually the plant strangles the life out of the tree. Gradually, it withers and dies (Palande).

Pleasure has the same kind of potential to take over our lives as the strangler fig. It can quickly cover our thoughts and motives. It can place a stranglehold on our wallets, our time, our priorities, our bodies, and our minds. We can become slaves to our own passions. The more pleasure we strive for, the emptier we feel, so we have to strive even more to reach a higher level of pleasure. We become pleasure junkies. The desire for pleasure keeps growing in our hearts and minds until we are completely encased in its clutches.

Long before Epicurus lived, Solomon created gardens and parks, amassed wealth, and collected a harem of beautiful women. He wrote in Ecclesiastes that he decided to test life with pleasure to find out what was good. But every pleasure proved to be meaningless. "I refused my heart no pleasure. My heart took delight in all my work, and this was the reward for all my labor. Yet when I surveyed all that my hands had done and what I had toiled to achieve, everything was meaningless, a chasing after the wind; nothing was gained under the sun" (Ecclesiastes 2:10-11).

Solomon experienced a wilderness of the soul even though there was plenty all around him. This wilderness took him completely by surprise. His writings in Ecclesiastes give us a good idea of his mental and spiritual condition, but can you imagine Solomon getting much empathy from anyone of his day? Or how about ours? Who would listen to his story and then say, "Poor Solomon, I wouldn't trade places with him for anything. He's got life so hard."? No, most people would think they could handle all the riches, all the pleasures, and all things that come with a life of ease. All most people want is a chance.

Yet Solomon's testimony was that the pursuit of pleasure as the first innate good strangled the life out of him. He chased every pleasure imaginable and discovered it was like chasing the wind. It ran him into a wilderness of the heart.

God is not against pleasure. Remember, it is God who created us as sensual beings with appetites and with desires, but God also created us as spiritual beings. Without being connected to God through Jesus, whom the New Testament calls the True Vine, we have less ability to discern holy pleasure from unholy pleasure. Our ability to find temperance and moderation in all things is compromised.

God wants us to find pleasure that is lasting. That is why we should seek holiness and set our hearts on things above. Pleasure is only one of the many aspects of holiness. St. Thomas Aquinas wrote: "The temperate man does not shun all pleasures, but those that are immoderate, and contrary to reason."[13]

It is not God's highest priority that we experience pleasure with every decision we make. Epicurus was wrong. Pleasure is not the first good innate in us. The first good innate in us is the desire to connect with the Highest Good, who grants us the wisdom to know when pleasure is profitable and when pleasure is vain.

Lent affords us the opportunity to evaluate whether we are chasing the wind. Traditionally, Christian leaders have encouraged us to deny certain pleasurable experiences during Lent in order to focus more clearly on the true source of happiness. Whether you do this or not, remember, God is not opposed to pleasure. God found pleasure in the creation and saw at the end of each day that "it was good." Yet pleasure was not the purpose of God's creative efforts, but rather a by-product.

During Lent, one goal is to allow God to show us those good and pleasurable things that produce happiness and are sustaining, as opposed to those things that last only a short period of time and are gone like the dew of the morning. Sometimes, it takes giving up some pleasures to discover that truth. That's part of the discipline of Lent.

Prayer

Our pleasure is in the Lord alone
And in His Good Creation
In mighty oaks and whispering pines
In deep forests and vast prairies
In raging waterfalls and gentle streams
In craggy mountainsides and soft sandy beaches

Our pleasure is in the Lord alone
And in His Mighty Hand
In phenomena and strange miracles
In tradition and transformation
In the grace of life's beginning and life's end
In the holding of His people

Our pleasure is in the Lord alone
And in His Son the Savior
In meals shared with the homeless
In embracing the sick and dying
In welcoming children
In serving, sacrificing, and saving

Our pleasure is in the Lord alone
And in His Kingdom Come
In worshiping without losing faith
In praying without losing hope
In giving without losing love
In singing without losing voice

Holy One, may our pleasure always be rooted in Your goodness and grace.
Amen.

Making Adjustments to Our Blind Spots
Lent 6

Have you ever been driving and were shocked to discover that there was another automobile right beside you in your blind spot? Most automobiles have an area where another automobile fails to appear in your side view mirror or in your peripheral vision.

Recently I discovered an exercise that demonstrates how common blind spots are. "Draw a square. About six inches to its right, draw a circle. Hold the image at arm's length and close your left eye. Focus on the square with your right eye, and slowly move the paper toward you. When the circle reaches your blind spot, it will disappear."[14]

Here's another version. Draw two bars that are separated by a space and in between the space is a circle. To the right of those bars draw a square. Close your right eye. With your left eye, look at the circle. Slowly move the paper closer to your face. At a certain distance, the bars will not look broken! Your brain has actually "filled in" the missing space (Eyes and Vision).

These little exercises prove that sometimes we actually see things that are not present, and sometimes we don't see things that are present. Strangely enough, this is reality. Not only is this true from a physiological point of view, but it is also true from a relational and a spiritual point of view. We all have blind spots in our relationships. We all have blind spots in our understanding of scripture and in living out our faith.

Take appearance, for example. We usually gravitate toward the tall rather than the short, the skinny rather than the overweight, the well-dressed rather than the unkempt, the beautiful or handsome rather than the homely.

When Samuel chose the first King for Israel, he chose Saul, "an impressive young man without equal among the Israelites—a head taller than any of the others" (1 Samuel 9:2). Saul turned out to be a dud. The next time God sent Samuel out to find a king, God told him not to consider the man's appearance or his height. "The Lord does not look at the things man looks at," he told Samuel. "Man looks at the outward appearance, but the Lord looks at the heart" (1 Samuel 16:7b).

Appearance is important, but it's not everything. Did Samuel have a blind spot? Did Saul's appearance persuade Samuel to choose him more than his character?

The formation of my denomination, the Southern Baptist Convention, grew out of a division between the Home Mission Society and the General Convention over the question of slavery. Most Baptists from the South believed the Bible supported the institution of slavery. Other Baptists, mostly from the North, differed on this issue. When a missionary from the South was denied an appointment on the mission field because he owned slaves, the wheels were greased for a split, hence the formation of the Southern Baptist Convention. Many Baptists of that day were blinded by their culture and a way of life that depended on the slaves for economic survival. Because of their blind spot, they could not see that the Bible supported the liberation of the slaves.

These two examples, one from the Bible, the other from more than 150 years ago in American history, are not unique. The truth is we all have blind spots in areas of relationships and scriptural interpretation.

Whenever we discover a new one, it ought to cause us to think about how many remain that we have not yet discovered.

This is not to say we cannot know truth. Jesus claimed to be the truth. To know Jesus is to know the truth, but this doesn't mean we can know all truth. Knowing all truth is not within our grasp. The apostle Paul said it like this: "Now we see but a poor reflection as in a mirror; then we shall see face to face. Now I know in part; then I shall know fully, even as I am fully known" (1 Corinthians 13:12).

We must be careful that we do not claim to know more than we know. For some people, this is their blind spot. They cannot see that when they proclaim to know all truth, they've just revealed what they cannot see—their own limitations. It can be difficult to admit that there are things we don't know and things we cannot know beyond all doubt. Not to admit this limitation leads to arrogance and dogmatism.

God sent Nathan the prophet to King David to confront David with his adulterous act with Bathsheba. David could not see that his sin was going to rot away his soul. David could not see the pain his decision would cause him, and also Bathsheba. David could not see that he had abused his power and taken advantage of a woman. David could not see that his morality as an individual had implications for his leadership of a nation. God sent Nathan the prophet to show David his blind spot. When the light was shone on David's blind spot, he repented.

On the contrary, the Pharisees did not repent when Jesus showed them their blind spots. On one occasion, he summed up their problem by telling these religious people that while they pointed out specks in the eyes of others, they had logs sticking out of their own. They were blinded by their own arrogance and the belief that they had access to all truth.

I have blind spots and you have them, too. We need to be willing to take a look at ourselves when others point out things they see in us. We may need to seek opinions from others so we can be as objective as possible. Should they be right, then changes in our behavior, positions, or beliefs need to follow.

It would be a great sin to be like the Pharisees, so cocksure we know all the answers that we fail to examine our lives in light of what the Lord and others see in us. As Socrates said while standing before the jury in the court of Athens in the year 399 B.C.E., "The unexamined life is not worth living."[15]

Imagine the foolishness of writing a book without submitting it to a proofreader. Imagine an architect not submitting his or her plans to the scrutiny of engineers. Imagine if engineers in Detroit never built prototypes of their cars and gave them test drives. Imagine if Boeing never did simulation flights of their planes or hired test pilots to fly new models before building their new line. Imagine a drug company that never tested new medications or if the FDA never did trials before releasing them to sell to the public. Yet how many of us live our lives without inviting anyone into our inner chambers to question motives, direction, commitments, goals, or values? How many of us remain accountable to absolutely no one? How many of us do very little self-evaluation? Is it any wonder so many of us end up in the wilderness?

During Lent, we invite the Holy Spirit into our lives for a check-up. We allow God's Spirit to purge us of old habits and release us from guilt. We learn to forgive ourselves for old sinful ways, embrace new spiritual disciplines, loosen old grudges, and lay down burdens that God should be carrying for us.

While this kind of evaluation might be done in isolation from others, we can also be open to listening to others, realizing that God uses others at times to speak to us. While we don't always have to take what people say to us as the gospel, the key is not to dismiss too quickly what others say they see in us.

The little exercises I mentioned earlier prove we have blind spots. Once we discover them or once they are revealed to us, what will we do about them? May we be humble enough to make the necessary adjustments, especially as it relates to our faith and how we live our faith before the Lord and others. Otherwise, we will become like the Pharisees—religious, but blind to our own sin.

The season of Lent can do us little good unless we acknowledge we have lived with blind spots and may be living with some now.

Spouses are often blind to the reality that they have stopped dating one another. Parents are often blind to the realization that they are not spending quality time with their children. It's not unusual for men to become blind that their career has become more important than their family. I've seen coaches at Little League yell and scream at their boys as if they were professional athletes instead of children who need praise and encouragement. I've seen many families who sacrificed weekend after weekend for sporting events with their children but would never consider volunteering their time for a community or church project.

Whenever I'm driving and a car moves out of my blind spot so that I see it, I am grateful. Seeing it helps me avoid danger.

As we move through Lent, pray that God will show us those issues of life that are in our blind spots. Unless we examine our lives and know what's there, how can we avoid danger and the downfalls that are common to us all?

Prayer

Lord of Light,

We have been deceiving ourselves in this wilderness. We have clung to our narrow-minded understanding and our limited vision. We have steered away from Your path to follow attractive mirages. We have become blind to Your way through our legalistic doctrines, confining creeds, social mores, political propaganda, trendy spiritualism, and patriotic ideals. We've become so focused on biblical law that we cannot see our own sin before us.

We confess, Lord, we really don't know all that much about life, about love, or about You. Transform us from lecturers into learners. Teach us Your ways; make them known to us. Remind us to take many stops along our journey to simply listen for You, and allow You to shed light on the areas to which we have become blind.

Amen.

Another Day Means Another Chance

Lent 7

What do these people have in common? A child who gets cut from the soccer team; a teenage boy who gets turned down when he asks a girl for a date; a man or woman who is passed over for a promotion; an elderly person who is told he or she can no longer live at home but must move to a retirement center. All these deal with some form of disappointment.

Disappointment is the failure to have expectations fulfilled. It is the loss of a dream. It comes from missed opportunities. It is hope that is no longer within our reach. A certain amount of grief is involved in disappointment.

Disappointment is a universal emotion. Only rarely does a person fail at something and not be disappointed. This may be because expectations were not very high in the first place. Usually, the higher our expectations, the greater our disappointment.

Every time a baseball player steps into the batter's box to try to hit a baseball, he knows the odds are against him. On average, a good player will get a hit twenty-five to thirty percent of the time. That makes for a lot of disappointing trips to the batter's box.

However, all good players go to the plate with optimism. What if the batter went to the plate thinking, "I'm a failure three-fourths of the time"? What are the chances the player would stay in the game very long?

What separates the good players from the bad ones, besides their natural talent and work ethic, is attitude. The one who learns to deal with disappointment constructively is the one who will have better self-esteem and will be the most successful at the game and at life.

Some people have a different remedy for disappointment—they don't expect anything. Since great expectations might lead to great disappointment, they just never live with much hope. This kind of outlook leads to mediocrity and underachievement.

Can you imagine a fisherman going to the lake without great expectations? What fisherman, disappointed from the last failed attempt at enticing a largemouth bass with a plastic worm, is going to park the boat and vow never to fish again? By nature, fishermen are optimistic people. They are also realists, or their sport wouldn't be called "fishing" but "catching."

Yet they go to the lake every time with lures, bait, rods, reels, and stringers. Of course optimism can be carried to an extreme. I bought a fish stringer once that measured twenty feet in length. It could hold a hundred or more bass and still have line left to play tug of war. Any man putting the boat in the water thinking he was going to fill up that stringer was sure to be disappointed.

When people carefully measure their expectations with the precision that a cook uses to measure a recipe, they can keep disappointment to a minimum while maintaining progress. I'm bound for disappointment if I think I could compete in a marathon. It's not beyond the realm of possibility if I trained for a year or more. However, setting my sights on running a mile or two is more realistic.

Sometimes disappointment is a sign that we are in the batter's box swinging away. That's much better than sitting on the sidelines as a spectator. Spectators bark out a lot of information and advice, but it's only those who are in the game who are growing and learning to be successful. Sometimes we have to ignore all the negative feedback or at least realize who is giving it.

So, the next time you are dealing with disappointment, pause long enough to pat yourself on the back and remind yourself that at least you are in the game. Then ask yourself, "Are my expectations realistic? If so, what can I do next time to increase my chances of success? If not, how can I set goals realistic enough to reach, but challenging enough to stretch me?"

People who do not deal well with disappointment will end up

wandering in the wilderness. Some end up there after their first major setback. Others end up there after two or three failures.

However, failure is a part of life. So is disappointment. Without experiencing these, we wouldn't be human. Those who have rarely experienced disappointment may not be better than you; they may simply be people who have not risked as much or they may not have set the bar very high.

Finding ourselves in the wilderness of failure or disappointment through no fault of our own isn't the worst place to be. We are in grave danger only when we lose our desire to make the effort to try again or to set our goals in different directions.

So when the world says "Batter up!"—pick up your pinewood and step into that batter's box. If you are going to go down, go down swinging. Or if baseball's not your game, change sports. Sometimes it's not the hit that makes us successful. Sometimes it's not whether we catch the bass that made the trip wonderful. Sometimes it's not the gold medal that makes us champions. Sometimes success is measured by a great attitude.

Disappointment is tempered when we acknowledge that the Lord has given us another day. Another day means we have another chance to lay it on the line and, therefore, another chance to succeed. It also means risking disappointment should we try again or try something different. But our efforts are worth the risk because if we expect nothing, nothing is what we'll get.

As this first week of Lent comes to an end, you may already be disappointed that you have not followed through with some of your disciplines this Lenten season. Some of the daily disciplines you vowed to work on may have already been challenged by the demands of the week. Some of the bad habits you wanted to give up may have already worked their way back into your day. If so, I can assure you that Satan has taken the opportunity to tell you that you are nothing but a big spiritual failure.

Hey, that's bull. Today is another day. Tomorrow's another opportunity. The Lord is already standing in tomorrow. When we get there, the Lord will be there, ready to greet us and give us another opportunity to make a difference.

Prayer

God of our todays and our tomorrows,

When today is difficult and filled with disappointments, when we recall our failed relationships, our lost hopes, our embarrassments, our bitterness, our grief, we want nothing more than to give up on our journey. We want nothing more than to let the wilderness grow up over us and bury our sad, sorry selves.

But each night You bring us the blessing of quiet rest. Each morning You offer a new resurrection. Remind us, Lord, that You are not just a God of this moment, but of all moments. You are constantly breathing life into all things. Take our disappointments of today and use them to give us wisdom, empathy, and grace for tomorrow.

Amen.

Only God Can Defeat Leviathan

Lent 8

When I was a boy there was a closet that was dark and cold in the middle of my grandparents' house. The door creaked when it was opened, and it looked like a place where a kid might get lost and fall into the dark abyss of the earth. My uncle told me that a "Booger Man" lived in there. I believed him. Of course, now I imagine he had something stashed in there that he didn't want a four-year-old to disturb.

In the television show *The Munsters*, Grandpa had a pet dragon named Spot that lived under the stairs. Every time the stairs were raised, Spot blew out a stream of fire that would singe your eyebrows, or worse. The Booger Man and Spot were little leviathans.

Technically, a little leviathan is an oxymoron. Little leviathans can actually be tamed. Even Spot the dragon was domesticated. A real leviathan cannot be tamed or domesticated. Leviathan is a mythological creature of the Bible and is the symbol of chaos. He is much like Lotan of Canaanite mythology, a seven-headed monster of the deep. Leviathan is too big, too ferocious, too Herculean, and too monstrous for any person to conquer.

A real Leviathan is not a little problem that can be worked out, a little fear that can be overcome, or a difficult relationship that can be smoothed out. A real Leviathan is a tsunami; it's a class five hurricane; it's an E5 tornado; it's an atomic bomb; it's September 11; it's suffering so great that death begins to look like a viable option; it's chaos that turns your world upside down and inside out, that threatens to consume you.

In the Bible, Job is engulfed in the clutches of the Leviathan. The reader is told that Job has done nothing to deserve the chaos in his life. After losing his possessions, wealth, servants, and all of his family, except his wife who soon after abandons him; after his friends turn on him; and after losing his health, Job pleads his case before God. He speaks boldly to God in protest until his lips tip the balance of his speech toward arrogance.

When God finally speaks to Job, He asks:

Can you pull in the Leviathan with a fishhook or tie down his tongue with a rope? Can you put a cord through his nose or pierce his jaw with a hook? Will he keep begging you for mercy? Will he speak to you with gentle words? Will he make an agreement with you for you to take him as your slave for life? Can you make a pet of him like a bird or put him on a leash for your girls?...No one is fierce enough to rouse him. Who then is able to stand against me? Who has a claim against me that I must pay? Everything under heaven belongs to me. (Job 41:1-5, 10-11)

Job then pulls back and realizes God is not obliged to do anything for him. He cannot make God do anything for him any more than he can tame Leviathan. Job then confesses that he believes God can do all things and that he spoke of things he did not understand, of things too wonderful for him to know (42:2-3).

Job learned through his suffering that he had nowhere to turn except to God and he had no more control over God's actions than he did the Leviathan's. He confessed that God could do all things and placed his belief in God despite the injustice of his suffering. Job knew that if the Leviathan were ever going to release its chaotic hold on his life, God was the only one who could control it and defeat it.

This is what the Psalmist believed:

But you, O God, are my king from of old; you bring salvation upon the earth. It was you who split open the sea by your power; you broke the heads of the monster in the waters. It was you who crushed the heads of Leviathan and gave him as food to the creatures of the desert. (Psalm 74:12-14)

Have you ever met Leviathan? Do you know someone who has? It's a terrible thing. We all deal with little "dragons," fears that keep us from exploring certain areas of our lives, little "Spots" that stay tucked away under stairs but breathe out fire from time to time. They threaten us but don't destroy us. We seem to keep going despite their nuisances. But we can feel powerless against real Leviathans: grief, depression, guilt, hopelessness, loss of self-worth, mounting debt, addictions, and certain temptations, to name just a few.

When Leviathan has us in his grips and all order seems to have escaped our lives, it will serve us well to look to the One who has defeated Leviathan and can bring us through our time of suffering or sinful indiscretions. We are not promised that we will come out unscathed. We are not even promised that we will understand the reason for our suffering or have restored to us what we have lost. However, within our disorganized, chaotic world, the God of order will come to us and speak to us. We should be ready to listen. Perhaps God will even speak out of the storm as He did to Job.

Whatever storms come our way and whatever monster rises from the deep seeking to claim us, we must remember that God will remain our refuge, our strength, and our salvation. We are on a spiritual journey during this season of Lent that can lead us to a place where we can see the Leviathan defeated. It can be done because Jesus rose from the dead. The same power that raised Jesus from the dead is available to help us defeat Leviathan.

If the Leviathan has dragged you into a wilderness, or is threatening to, you can take heart today and claim victory that God will not allow the Leviathan to win the battle in your life. You, of course, play a role in this battle. Yield to Jesus. Submit to Him. Allow the Lord to defeat the enemy for you. Surrender your will to Him. Then the words of Isaiah will come true: "In that day, the Lord will punish with his sword, his fierce, great and powerful sword, Leviathan the gliding serpent, Leviathan the coiling serpent; he will slay the monster of the sea" (Isaiah 27:1).

I remind you that it took some time for Job to journey through his wilderness before God slew his Leviathan, but God was faithful. God will be faithful in your case, too.

Have faith in God. Continue to journey with Him. Continue to live with the hope that God will close the jaws of the Leviathan in your life as He has in the lives of others.

Prayer

Mighty One,

Some of us seek out the wilderness, hoping for adventure. Some of us stumble upon these desolate places when we have been lost for a while. And some of us are violently thrown into these deep dark places by a Leviathan, without any warning. Only You can save us!

We are fighting in this wilderness, desperately trying to claw our way free of the monsters that have ensnared us—our Leviathans called shame, disease, depression, grief, loneliness, pain, anger, addiction, and unexplainable suffering. We are losing the battle fighting on our own, and we grow weary too quickly. Only You can release us! Only You can show us a way out!

Strengthen our faith, Lord. Keep us walking beside You on our journey through the wilderness. Give us the wisdom to hand our swords over to You, and let You battle the Leviathans we are too weak to fight on our own.

Amen.

Loving People as Subjects, Not Objects

Lent 9

In his book, *The Lord Is My Shepherd*, Harold Kushner tells about Martin Buber, a German philosophy professor of the early 20th century. One day a young student came to see him, deeply concerned about a draft notice he had received to serve in the German army during World War I. A pacifist by nature, the young man was afraid of being killed in battle. At the same time, he had a deep love for his country. He didn't like the thought of someone else dying in his place, either. He didn't know what to do, so he went to Buber for help.

The young man caught Buber at a bad time. He was working through a difficult theological-philosophical problem and was annoyed by the young man's claim on his time. He said something along the lines of "That's a serious dilemma; do what you think is right." The conversation was brief and the young man left.

It wasn't long afterward that Buber received word that the young man had committed suicide. Buber was drenched in guilt. He wondered if the young man's fate would have been different if he had responded differently to him. He realized that he had treated the young man as an object, not as a subject. He had not treated the young man as a person of worth, as someone who deserved his time and attention.

The experience led Buber to think about how people typically relate to one another. He concluded that we either relate to other people in an *I–Thou* or in an *I–It* relationship. In an *I–It* relationship, we treat people as objects. We are primarily concerned with how we can use the other person to meet our needs. Others' needs or issues are of no concern to us.

For example, imagine you are in a restaurant and the waitress comes over to take your order. The waitress gets your order confused. She seems distracted during your meal. She forgets to bring the ketchup you asked for. She brings unsweetened tea instead of the sweet tea you requested. Her service is lousy, and you are thinking that your dissatisfaction will be reflected in the size of your tip. You might even complain to the management. You relate to the waitress in an I-It relationship. The only concern you have for her is whether she met your needs during the meal.

Buber says that the other way we interact with people is in an *I–Thou* relationship. In this relationship we see the other person as a subject, someone who has needs and feelings of his or her own which are of concern to us.

Consider the encounter with the waitress. You could relate to her differently. Instead of seeing her as an object, Buber says you could see her as a subject. You could call her by name; after all, she wears her name on her uniform. Her name tag says, "I am a person. See me as more than just a waitress."

You could say something like this: "Brenda, I've noticed you are struggling to keep up with all our requests this evening. Have you had a long day?" You never know when a simple question like that will give others the opportunity to lay a burden down, if only for a moment. You might be the first person of the day who cared enough to look past the uniform and see a real person and ask a caring question.

Jesus treated people as subjects, not objects. One example is the story of Zacchaeus, the tax collector. As Jesus passed through Jericho, Zacchaeus ran ahead of Him and climbed in a sycamore tree so he could see Jesus coming.

> *When Jesus reached the spot, He looked up and said to him, "Zacchaeus, come down immediately. I must stay at your house today." So he came down at once and welcomed him gladly. All the people saw this and began to mutter, "He has gone to be the guest of a 'sinner'"* (Luke 19:5-7).

The Romans saw Zacchaeus as an object. They didn't care anything about him as a person. All they cared was that he collected taxes from the people. The Jewish people saw Zacchaeus as an object. They didn't care to know anything about him because he didn't care anything about them. He cared only about becoming rich by levying heavy taxes upon them and becoming rich at their expense. Zacchaeus saw the people as objects of taxation, nothing more.

But Jesus saw Zacchaeus as a subject, someone of worth, and someone who needed a friend. Because Jesus cared about Zacchaeus as an individual, his life was changed.

> *But Zacchaeus stood up and said to the Lord, "Look, Lord! Here and now I give half of my possessions to the poor, and if I have cheated anybody out of anything, I will pay back four times the amount." Jesus said to him, "Today salvation has come to this house, because this man, too, is a son of Abraham. For the Son of Man came to seek and to save what was lost." (Luke 19:8-10)*

It's easy for us to define our neighbor in narrow terms instead of the way Jesus desires. Once we make the changes in ourselves, we might be surprised at the changes we can make in the lives of others when we look at people as subjects and not objects. Much of what the world defines as love is nothing more than one person treating the other person as an object. Many men treat women nicely in the beginning of a relationship only to throw them away after they get what they want. Of course, it works both ways.

There are many Zacchaeuses out there, people who have been treated in an *I-It* manner in most of their relationships. These people are wandering around in a wilderness. They are lost and trying to find anyone who will love them and have an interest in their lives for the right reasons.

Hungry for love, they latch on to people for the wrong reason, sometimes thinking they are being loved, only to be disappointed and wounded. Each time, their trust level in others drops.

It takes time to earn the trust of these people and to demonstrate a different kind of relationship, the one Buber called an *I-Thou* relationship. Real love happens in these relationships. We love not for what we hope to get in return, but we love because we have learned that love of this kind is the glue that holds the world together. Love of this kind has the potential to change a person's heart. Love of this kind is what ultimately makes us happy. It is the kind of love that Jesus has for us. It is the kind of love that 1 Corinthians 13:5 speaks about when it says "[love] is not self-seeking."

Once people understand that we are offering this kind of love without expectation, that it's free but not cheap, and that it's genuine, we will help them leave their wilderness.

Today, you will likely encounter someone who is walking in a wilderness, but you might not even know it. The more people you treat as subjects, the better chance you have of opening up a new door in a person's day, reminding him or her that he or she is a person of worth, a person that God loves, and a person who has something of worth to offer this world.

Prayer

Christ our Counselor,

We confess our inability to love our neighbors. In every relationship, we seek self-serving benefits. We want love, respect, understanding, and forgiveness from others, yet we don't offer these gifts freely in return. We are accustomed to treating others as objects, mere things that exist to serve our needs or entertain us. And when we encounter those who are unable to serve our needs, we toss them aside, discounting their value.

But You, Jesus, have taught us that every human has inherent value through being made in the image of the Father. Teach us to see our neighbors through Your eyes. Lessen our neediness and increase our service. Give us opportunities to treat others as subjects, people with their own stories. Help us engage in the stories of others, offering Your love, respect, understanding and forgiveness, so that they may want to become a part of your Great Story.

Amen.

Turning Trash
into Triumph
Lent 10

While on vacation in North Carolina, I threw an important piece of paper in the trashcan in my hotel room. Later, when I realized I still needed the information on the paper, I discovered the maid had already emptied the trashcan.

When I found the maid, she was about halfway down the hall in her cleaning regimen. I approached her to ask whether I could look through the trash to find my lost information. This hard-working woman knew very little English. She offered me an ice bucket and an extra trash bag, but we never got much beyond that.

The hotel maintenance man proved to be a better source. He showed me where the maid had already taken the trash from the rooms she had cleaned during the morning. He was kind enough to pull out two large bags of hotel trash. Then, one by one, I opened up individual bags from the rooms, and I began trying to identify my own trash. Disgusting.

The experience reminded me that we've all got trash in our lives, every one of us—no exceptions. We don't like the trash we create, though. We discard it as soon as we can before it starts to smell. We prefer not to look at it again or handle it again. It's too messy.

Trash reminds us of our mistakes and of our humanity. That's not such a bad thing, except that humanity has its nasty side. In case you have forgotten, just think how we start out as babies. We get nasty when left to ourselves. We would stay nasty if we did not have some loving individual who cared enough to clean us up.

As adults, we celebrate the independence our children exude when they insist on doing things for themselves. We don't want children dependent on us forever. As children grow older, they learn to take care of themselves, to clean themselves up. However, this individualism has its limitations and its drawbacks.

As I opened the first bag of trash, I found beer bottles, an empty pizza box, old newspapers, more beer bottles, leftover soap; nope, that's not my trash. Another bag revealed empty soda cans, a half-eaten Subway sandwich, tourist information, an empty shoebox, leftover soap; nope, that's not my trash. I went through bag after bag of trash.

Weeding through the trash of that dumpster, I noticed I could quickly eliminate some of the bags of trash that were not mine. But I had to open up others and pick through them for a moment or two before I eliminated them.

Sometimes other people's trash looked a lot like my own. Then I came across a bag of trash that contained an empty Doritos bag, an empty Lay's Potato Chip bag, two wadded up pieces of paper, an empty Capri-Sun container, two wadded up photographs, and some leftover soap; hey, that looks like my trash! While my trash might not be the same as your trash, trash is trash.

That's the way it is with sin. Sin is sin. Some of my sin is easily distinguishable from yours. Some of my sin looks a lot like yours, and some of yours looks a lot like mine. This is the reason the season of Lent is a season of spiritual discipline that should not have denominational bounds. This spiritual season isn't just for Catholics, Methodists, Episcopalians, Baptists, Presbyterians, or a host of other denominations. It's a season for spiritual reflection and discipline for anyone preparing for the Passion Week and Easter.

Picking through the trash of that dumpster reminded me that each day I need to try to identify my own trash. I can't do anything about anybody else's trash. It does me no good to point out the trash you've got in your life. That's what Jesus corrected the Pharisees for doing: "Stop talking about that speck of trash you see in your brother's eye while you've got a garbage truck load of it in your own eye," He said (paraphrase of Matthew 7:3). Though it can be a messy process, it is important to identify our own trash.

Each of us produces our own trash in life. Trash is a by-product of living. However, trash that is not dealt with properly can dam up the waterways of life and pollute the quality of living that God intended for us to enjoy. More than that, trash can block our relationship with God and with others and cut off the blessings from God that He wants to flow freely to us.

The Bible calls the trash we produce "sin." Sin is something we all have in our lives: "For all have sinned and fall short of the glory of God" (Romans 3:23 NKJV). And "if we say that we have not sinned, we make Him a liar, and His word is not in us" (1 John 1:10 NKJV).

So what are we to do about this sin issue? Can't we just throw it away and say, "I'm through with this sin and I'm not going to do it anymore"?

I wish it were that easy. I wish I had that much willpower. Perhaps you can do that with a few things, but you cannot do that with sin in general. You cannot simply decide to stop sinning any more than a baby can decide to stop getting a diaper dirty.

I doubt it pays very much, but if you want a steady job, be a trash collector. I can with all certainty declare that there will never be a shortage of trash in this world. With certainty, you can empty the wastebasket today, but it will fill up again soon.

You can say, "I sinned today, but I'll do better tomorrow." With certainty, when tomorrow comes, with it will come more opportunities to sin. Though we may overcome many of the temptations that confront us, we are sure to fail in some of them. I only offer you our track record as proof that we are a hopeless lot left to our own strength, our own ability to make decisions, and our own ability to clean up our act. This is why we must take advantage of the opportunity we have to prepare ourselves for Easter. We need it. For many of us, we've allowed trash to accumulate.

As I made my way through the hotel trash looking for the important piece of paper I had discarded, it suddenly hit me that there was some irony in that trash. Every little trash bag thrown out of each hotel room and placed in that dumpster contained soap. Something designed to keep us clean was mixed in with the nasty, messy, smelly trash of that dumpster.

The irony lived out in the lives of many people is that they realize they've got trash in their lives, but they feel as long as they do a few things to clean up their act, everything will end up fine. Some people try to patronize God by showing up at church a few times a year, by giving a few dollars to charity or doing some good deeds, or simply by living a good, decent life.

Many people will compare their lives to others and say, "Well, I know I'm no saint, but I know I am a better person than some of those people who go to church on a regular basis." Since they don't think their trash smells as bad as someone else's, they think they must be okay. Unfortunately, they are comparing themselves to the wrong person. The standard by which we should measure our lives is the life of Jesus Christ. Place your life against the standard of Jesus' life. How do you measure up?

Jesus set the bar and when we try to clean up our act on our own, we are guaranteed to find ourselves in a wilderness. We will stay in the wilderness as long as we believe we can please Jesus simply by living a good life, doing enough good deeds, or being better than most people.

God's standard is no less than perfection! If God requires that sin be destroyed, eradicated, removed from our lives; should we just give up? Well, yeah. That's exactly what we should do. We should give up. We should surrender our lives to the Lord. We should acknowledge that we are defeated, that we are unable to defeat sin in our lives without the Lord.

God requires an acknowledgment that we need Jesus for that purpose. God requires that we seek Jesus as our Savior, an act of submission and humility. Until we get to a point where we are willing to submit our will to God, our money to God, our occupation to God, our family to God, our dating life to God, our Saturday night activities to God, our free time to God and what we do, what we read, what we see on the Internet, and where we go to God, we are going to continue to make trash and haul it into our wilderness.

One of the most important self-discoveries comes when we are sitting amid our own trash, whether great or small, and realize that we cannot clean it up on our own; nor is there anyone else other than the Lord who has the power to clean up the trash in our lives.

When our trash is due to our sin, the Lord's promise is this: "If we confess our sins, He is faithful and just to forgive us our sins and to cleanse us from all unrighteousness" (1 John 1:9 NKJV).

Not all of our trash is due to our sin. Sometimes people dump their trash on our lawns. We are left to deal with it, and we often discover we are not so good at sorting through it. We can be consumed by it. We can get lost in anger, revenge, and bitterness. We find we still need God's help.

Oh, by the way, among the trash of that dumpster, I found that important piece of paper I had thrown away. It was a messy job, but I looked and looked until I found it, and then I celebrated.

God is like that. He searches for us among the mess of this world, some of which we've created and some of which others have created. Yet God believes we are worth saving, so He doesn't give up on us.

Without God, our trash eventually leads to tragedy. With the power of God, our trash is turned into triumph. That's the message of the resurrection! That's the message of the Christian faith! That is the Gospel!

Prayer

Divine Deliverer,

When we contemplate our sin, this wilderness begins to resemble a landfill. We think we can hide our sin deep down so others don't know it's there. But soon the putrid rottenness seeps up into the topsoil. Sin cannot be hidden, especially from You. We cannot pretend it away.

Sin is among us, in us, tempting us, directing us all hours of the day. We cannot escape its shadow; we cannot deny its power.

Merciful God, thank You for understanding our dilemma. Thank You for recognizing how much we suffer and how we allow others to suffer under our sin. Thank You for sending us a Savior to free us from these heavy burdens and to live as an example of true righteousness and purity.

Give us a clear vision of our sin each day so that we may always turn to Christ for help. Fill us with the knowledge that we do not have to bow down to this trash heap any longer. Remind us of our total dependence on Jesus to get us out of this landfill, and let us have the humility to grasp His outstretched arm.

Amen.

Going "All-In" for the Lord

Lent 11

I enjoy playing cards, but I've never played poker. When you mention "chips," I think about food, that television show from the '70s with the motorcycle cops, Ponch and Jon, and cow pies.

A royal flush sounds like something a king does after going to the bathroom. Three of a kind is easy enough to understand, but I don't know if that hand beats a full house. However, I'm slowly becoming educated about poker because I watch it on television sometimes. It's broadcast like a heavyweight-boxing match that has more than two boxers in the ring. The poker bout isn't over until there's only one person left standing, the one with all the chips.

When I saw my first hand of poker on television, outside of a Western movie, I couldn't understand what was so interesting about watching other people play cards. But after watching a few hands of Texas Hold'em, I began to be seduced by the drama of each flip of the card. I was intrigued by the strategy of the players and their ability to maintain poker faces and mislead their opponents by betting on worthless hands. I began to see how easily one can be pulled into a gambling world.

While entertaining, these shows are seductively dangerous. They show only matches where people win money. Even the losers walk away from the table with lots of money. They never show the young college student who has managed to tap into his college fund and honestly believes that the next $1000 tournament he enters will make him into an instant celebrity and a rich person. They never show the father who squanders the family's savings because he's become addicted to high stakes card games.

Like many things in this world that look innocent, this one is encumbered with dangers. In an Associated Press article on teenage gambling, Ed Looney, head of the New Jersey Gambling Council on Compulsive Gambling, stated that fifteen percent of all teenagers who play poker will develop some gambling problems and five percent will become addicted. When betting is involved, it's not an innocent game.[16]

With this as a disclaimer, I want to use one of poker's most exciting bets to illustrate the kind of life that the Lord wants us to live. You can learn something from everything, even from a game of poker.

As a player looks at his cards during a hand of poker to make some determination on how many of his chips to bet, he may decide to bet them all, at which time all the chips are pushed to the middle of the table and the player says, "I'm all-in."

Such a play may force the opponent to fold, giving up all the chips that have been bet on his hand up until that time, or the opponent may match the number of chips that have been bet. If the chips are matched, the dealer lays down the flop (three cards are dealt) from which each player seeks to build a hand along with his two cards. The final card, called the River card, is then laid down. The player with the best hand from these four cards plus his two cards wins the pot. If the player who is "all-in" wins, he plays on. If he loses, the game is over, as he has no more chips with which to play.

Christians worship a God who wants us to play our hand in life with this kind of abandonment. God wants us to live with an "all-in" attitude. The great temptation is to play our hand much closer to the vest. Often, we want to place only a few of our chips on the line for God and hold a large number back to place in other areas of life.

Jesus said that the greatest commandment is to "love the Lord your God with ALL your heart and with ALL your soul and with ALL your mind and with ALL your strength" (Mark 12:30; emphasis added).

Once a man came up to Jesus and asked what he must do to inherit eternal life. Jesus quoted several of the Ten Commandments to him. The man told Jesus he'd kept them since he was young. Jesus then told him to go sell all of his possessions and give to the poor and then he would have treasure in heaven. After that, he could be His disciple.

Jesus wanted the man to be "all-in." He wanted the man to put all of his chips in the center of God's will. Jesus knew a poker face when he saw one. Although the man said he'd been keeping all the commandments, Jesus called his hand. When the young man heard Jesus' call, he folded. He walked away "because he had great wealth" (Matt. 19:22). He wanted to keep all his chips.

Contrast this story with one Mark tells in his gospel. Jesus and His disciples went to the temple where they watched the crowd bring their money and place it in the temple treasury. When the copper coins hit the collection boxes, they made lots of noise. It wasn't much of a secret which worshipers gave large sums of money and which ones didn't. However, no one could know who really gave sacrificially, except for Jesus.

When a widow came and dropped two small copper coins in the treasury, worth only a fraction of a penny, Jesus pointed her out to His disciples: "I tell you the truth, this poor widow has put more into the treasury than all the others. They all gave out of their wealth; but she, out of her poverty, put in everything—all she had to live on" (Mark 12:43-44).

This woman was "all-in." She had cast her lot totally with God, depending totally and completely upon God to take care of her and supply her needs.

Jesus knelt down in the garden of Gethsemane. Falling with His face to the ground, He prayed, "My Father, if it is possible, may this cup be taken from me. Yet not as I will, but as you will" (Matt. 26:39). Jesus was faced with the brutality of the cross. It was not the hand He wanted to play. God had dealt Him a king to be sure. But this king came with a crown of thorns. It was a great temptation for Jesus to fold.

Nearby, His disciples slept. Among them was a disciple named Peter, a well-meaning disciple who loved Jesus. Jesus had predicted the hand he would play that very night. It would be a hand most poker players would die for, three of a kind. That's exactly what Peter told Jesus He'd do, die for Him. Yet the three of a kind came in three separate denials; three times he'd deny he knew Jesus.

While Jesus rebuffed Satan's temptation to call twelve legions of angels to rescue Him from the hands of the Roman soldiers, Peter was drawing three of a kind on the flop. While Jesus made a commitment in the Garden of Gethsemane to be "all-in" for the sake of all humanity, Peter was hearing the rooster crow by the time the River card was laid down. The waters that flowed from this card were the bitter tears of a man with a broken heart who knew he'd forsaken his best friend.

Life is filled with choices. We all take risks of one kind or another. But every person who chooses not to go "all-in" for Jesus takes a huge gamble, although many are blind to it. Many who have acquired fame, prestige, money, assets, a great name, and the pleasures of this world, without going "all-in" for Jesus, see no benefit in laying all they have on the line for the Lord. They seem to have done quite well for themselves without His help. So they feel quite smug in holding onto their pile of chips, not realizing the risk they are taking.

Like the young man who wanted eternal life but not at the expense of giving up his earthly wealth, many people look for a religion that will allow them to play their hands on their own terms. So the bets are off when it comes to going "all-in."

To people who have such a philosophy of life, Jesus has some sobering words:

> "If anyone would come after me, he must deny himself and
> take up his cross and follow me. For whoever wants to save
> his life will lose it, but whoever loses his life for me will find
> it. What good will it be for a man if he gains the whole
> world, yet forfeits his soul?" (Matt. 16:24-26).

Peter wandered in a wilderness for several days. The burden upon him was heavy. Thankfully, he didn't end his life in despair like Judas.

Judas played his hand just as he wanted. He traded a king for thirty pieces of silver. The only problem was that once Judas had his money and the Romans had the king (Jesus), Judas was overcome with guilt and the realization that he'd made the wrong call. The guilt and despair became so great that he took his own life.

Redemption came for Peter after the resurrection of Jesus. Peter met Jesus by the Sea of Galilee. On three occasions Jesus asked Peter if he loved Him. Translation: "Peter, are you going to go 'all-in' for me with the rest of your life? If so, then take care of my sheep; that is, put your life in the middle of the needs of the people just as I have." Peter made that commitment.

When we do that, don't we stand to lose a lot? Yes. Jesus lost His life. James, Jesus' disciple, lost his. Outside biblical accounts indicate that most, if not all, of the other disciples lost their lives. It's reported that Peter was crucified upside down, believing that he was unworthy to die in the same manner as Jesus.

In many ways, we are supposed to lose our lives, too. We don't become martyrs, though a few might, but we are supposed to give up control of our lives to God, doing as God asks, going where God sends, and giving as God directs.

The great irony is this: the degree to which we decide to go "all-in" for Jesus is the degree of freedom we will discover. Those who decide to go "all-in" for the Lord learn that such a decision is really no gamble at all. It's a sure thing. Every person who's ever gone "all-in" has discovered this freedom, found the purpose of living, and received the gifts of abundant and eternal life.

This is not to say that life becomes easy. Jesus' life and the life of the disciples counter that suggestion. It is to say that life becomes meaningful. It is to say that life becomes purposeful and fruitful.

The great gamble is for those who really make no gamble at all, but play their hand close to the vest, holding back, afraid to go "all-in" for Jesus for a variety of reasons. We create our own wildernesses this way.

If you've been holding back on the Lord, Lent could have great meaning for you this year if you have enough faith to go "all in." Are there any areas of your life that you keep holding back for yourself? To which areas of your life have you not allowed Jesus access? Are you willing to push all your life into the middle of God's kingdom and say, "Lord, I'm all in"?

Prayer

All-Encompassing Messiah,
You demand all of us,
Our hearts in all that we love,
Our souls in all that we believe,
Our minds in all that we think,
Our strength in all that we do.

It is not easy to let go of the hands we are dealt,
Our triumphs or tribulations,
Our wealth or want,
Our delight or devastation,
Because we fear that's all there is for us in this life.

But You have made Your gracious presence known to us
And shown us that we are not alone in this wilderness.
You have laid down Your own life,
So we can lay down our cards before You.
Help us to go "all in" for You, Jesus.
Take away our fears so that we may
Boldly and completely give ourselves over to You. Amen.

A Friend Who Sticks Closer Than a Brother

Lent 12

For many years the number one show on television was NBC's *Friends*. This comedy is about six close-knit young friends, three men and three women, who live in New York City, frequently gathering at each other's apartments to share conversation. The show ran for eleven seasons.

The success of the show reflected a primal need for most people, to connect with others on more than a superficial level. People need friends, and most people feel the need to befriend others.

Warning: Not everyone who wants to spend time with you is a true friend. Sometimes, it takes adversity and difficult times to weed out the fair-weather friends from the real ones.

One of Jesus' most popular parables highlights this truth. A son came to his father and asked if he could have his share of the inheritance. Surprisingly the father gave his son his inheritance and the son left home. He lived the life of a wild bachelor. He had plenty of "friends" to help him spend his money. When his money ran out, so did his friends. More bad fortune followed. About the same time his money ran out, there was a famine throughout the land.

The young man found a job feeding swine, one of the worst imaginable jobs for a Jew, as the Jews considered these animals unclean. He was so hungry he would have eaten the husks he fed the swine. He decided that the servants at his father's house lived better than he was living, so he returned home in hopes that his father might at least allow him to return as a servant. To his surprise, the father welcomed him home! He called the servants to bring a robe and shoes for his son. He put a ring on his finger and ordered the servants to kill the fatted calf. He celebrated the return of a son who had been lost but now was found!

The experience must have taught the young man several lessons about real friendship. Those who are willing to forgive us of our mistakes are true friends. Those who are willing to sacrifice for us are true friends. A true friend can be trusted explicitly. A true friend will help us bear our burdens. A true friend will not abandon us when times are tough.

There will always be people hanging around when we are popular, successful, and healthy. If we throw our money around, we will always have people around us, but it may not be until the difficult times come that we discover who our real friends are.

I exchanged letters with a man in prison several years ago. On one occasion I asked him how many of his "friends" he did drugs with and hung out with had written, called, or come to see him. He wrote back, "Not one."

A proverb of Theophrastus says: "True friends visit us in prosperity only when invited, but in adversity they come without invitation."[17] A true friend will not abandon us when times are tough.

I once read that false friends are like our shadows. They keep close to us while we walk in the sunshine, but leave us when we cross into the shade.

The prodigal son discovered his father was his true friend because in the darkest moment of his life, his father did not abandon him. Jesus' parable has deeper meanings. Here is one of them: God is like the father in this story. We are like the prodigal. Most of us have been in places we shouldn't have been, doing things we shouldn't have done, with people we shouldn't have been involved with, only to discover when the good times were no more, neither were those we thought were our friends. The good news of this parable is that God is still our friend and is waiting for us to put our trust in Him, even after we have wasted in the wilderness much of what we've been given. God stands ready to welcome us home if we will humble ourselves and go.

Through Jesus, we have come to know God as a God full of grace, quick to forgive, slow to become angry, and always ready to celebrate our coming home.

Proverbs 18:24 says that "a man of many companions may come to ruin, but there is a friend who sticks closer than a brother."

Typically, most of us will befriend only those people we like, those people who give us some kind of benefits in return for our friendship. That's human nature. The uncommon friend is the one who gets little or nothing in return for his or her friendship other than the satisfaction of being Jesus to someone.

There are people who have lost their way in this world. They are wandering in a wilderness. They may have brought much of it on themselves. They might have had some bad luck. Regardless of their circumstances, the fact remains that they have few friends. We cannot rescue those who don't want to be rescued. We can't solve the deep conditions people have worked themselves into over time. We cannot fix in a day or a week what has taken someone a lifetime to become. However, we can be a friend. We can walk out into their wilderness and meet them.

If we spend a little time in the wilderness with them, seeing life from their perspective, they will know we are a true friend. Being able to understand life from their perspective will help us know how we can help meet their needs.

Jesus once asked, "What do you think? If a man owns a hundred sheep, and one of them wanders away, will he not leave the ninety-nine on the hills and go to look for the one that wandered off?" (Matthew 18:12).

Recovering alcoholics often make great friends to people lost in a world of alcoholism. Mothers who became pregnant out of wedlock and raised a child successfully with or without a father present often make great friends to a young teenager who has received the news she is pregnant. People who have dropped out of high school but returned to get a GED and found employment make great friends to high school dropouts who don't see the need for education.

People who have had marital problems, but found help in counseling and strengthened their marriage, can be good friends to couples who are constantly fighting or whose marriage has lost its life and passion. People who have gone through a divorce and eventually found a life of peace and happiness again can be good friends to people who are entering the early stages of life after a divorce.

When God gives us a friend, God gives us hope. You can become someone's hope. The thing about friendship is that we don't always know how much our friendship might mean to someone because we don't always know just how deep in the wilderness they might be walking.

Prayer

Compassionate Jesus,

You give hope to the hopeless, You bring peace to the troubled, and You give pardon to the guilty. In our wilderness, You walk beside us; You help us up when we stumble; You give us shelter during storms; You listen to our stories. Your light guides us home when we are tired of wandering, and You welcome us back with open arms. You are a true friend, Lord. Let Your example reside in us. May we all be a friend to those who have none, showing them Your love and light. Amen.

Singing
in the Rain
Lent 13

The 1952 movie *Singing in the Rain* has what has been called the single most memorable dance number on film. The film starred Gene Kelly, Donald O'Connor, and Debbie Reynolds. In the movie, the characters played by Kelly and Reynolds, Don Lockwood and Kathy Selden, fall in love. In the dance scene, Don kisses Kathy goodnight as the rain falls. She says, "This California dew is just a little heavier than usual tonight." "Really," says Don, "from where I stand the sun is shining all over the place."[18]

As Kathy goes inside, Don walks down the sidewalk, folds up his umbrella, and dances in the rain. He swings from lampposts and splashes in rain puddles. He is filled with joy and happiness. He sings: "I'm laughing at clouds/So dark up above/The sun's in my heart/And I'm ready for love/Let the storm clouds chase/Everyone from the place/Come on with the rain/I've a smile on my face/I walk down the lane/With a happy refrain/Just singin'/Singin' in the rain."[19]

The book of Acts tells a story about Paul and Silas. They were arrested in the city of Philippi for preaching the Gospel. After being beaten, they were thrown into prison. Even so, "about midnight Paul and Silas were praying and singing hymns to God" (Acts 16:25). They were bruised. They were cut. They were bleeding. They were in pain. The circumstances were far from pleasant. Yet in their hearts, Paul and Silas were rejoicing. Hymns bubbled from their hearts and flowed to their lips as they sang during the night. They were singing in the rain.

Haven't you known people who were able to rise above difficult circumstances that would cause the average person to be emotionally distraught or at least discouraged?

Jesus began His ministry with a trip into the wilderness where He was tempted for forty days. That doesn't sound like a trip to Disney World. It's likely that many who are reading this are walking through some kind of wilderness experience, although few of us do so by choice. Wilderness experiences are usually imposed on us, as in the case of Paul and Silas. However, the wilderness does not have the final say on our attitude. Luke, the writer of Acts, says that when Paul and Silas were singing, "the other prisoners were listening to them" (Acts 16:25). Imagine the reaction they must have had. There's no doubt they listened in disbelief after what had happened to Paul and Silas and asked themselves, "How could they still have an attitude of joy?"

When adversity, change, and hardships come our way, people are naturally curious about how we will respond. Will our words be bitter or will our words reflect the spirit of Christ? Will we curse God or will our words continue to praise God? People will be listening for our response.

One of the more amazing things about this story is how soon after being flogged and thrown into prison Paul and Silas were singing and influencing others. It doesn't take long to influence others. People quickly notice what kind of spirit we have within us. When adversity comes, it is an opportunity to demonstrate God's power and guidance in our lives. It's an opportunity to influence others for Christ.

George Stewart wrote: "Weak men are the slaves of what happens. Strong men are masters of what happens. Weak men are victims of their environment. Strong men are victors in any environment. Strong men may not change the circumstances, but they will use them, compel them to serve, and bend them to their purposes. They may not be able to change the direction of the wind, but somehow they will coerce the wind to fill their sails while they drive the tiller over to keep their course."[20]

Paul and Silas epitomized Stewart's words. Their songs gushed out of their spirit because their hearts were full of doxology and love, even after the men were arrested, flogged, and thrown into prison. They could sing in the rain because the Lord Jesus reigned in their hearts. The power given them from the Lord helped them rise above their situation.

Later their singing was interrupted by an earthquake.

The ground shook, releasing the fetters that held the prisoners in their cells. Surprisingly, no one tried to escape. Why? Because they were influenced by Paul and Silas. They were willing to follow the lead of a couple of men they had just met. Paul and Silas convinced everyone to remain where they were. Had they escaped on the jailer's watch, he likely would have been put to death. He actually drew his sword to kill himself before he was stopped by Paul and Silas.

The jailer was consumed with his problems, while Paul and Silas rose above theirs with the help of the Lord. It is human nature to become consumed with our problems. When it happens, we feel great pain and grief. Laments have a great purpose in our religious life. A lament is a way for us to express our deep pain, grief, and anger about our condition. Sometimes we have to move through a time of lament before we can find our way to an attitude of joy. It is the Spirit of the living God that enables us to rise above the pain and sing in the rain.

The jailer, after seeing their faith and courage, as well as hearing the unbelievable good news Paul and Silas had for him, then asked what he must do to be saved. They replied,

"Believe in the Lord Jesus, and you will be saved—you and your household." Then they spoke the word of the Lord to him and to all the others in his house. At that hour of the night the jailer took them and washed their wounds; then immediately he and all his family were baptized. The jailer brought them into his house and set a meal before them; he was filled with joy because he had come to believe in God—he and his whole family. (Acts 16:31-34)

We usually have no choice about the adversity we face, but we are always left with a choice of how we will respond. The way we respond could make the difference in convincing others that Jesus is sufficient to meet their needs. But first, we must believe that He is sufficient to meet our needs. When people see us dancing in the rain, they will want to know, how under the circumstances, we can swing from lampposts and splash in puddles. We can tell them that, while we may be saddened by what life has brought to us, our joy is not contingent upon our circumstances, but on the fact that the Lord Jesus is with us always.

During this season of Lent, whether we are walking through a self-imposed wilderness or whether we are faced with a very deep and personal crisis, may our spirits still reflect the joy of a risen Savior! The goal isn't to live in denial of any sad, difficult, tragic, or depressing news, but rather to keep it from having the last word. That's one of the messages of Easter: tragedy didn't have the last word. That's why we can live with hope. That's why we can swing from lampposts and splash in puddles even when the rain is falling.

Prayer

In the wilderness,
The sky is dark.
The shadows loom.
The air is thick and stale.
There are promises broken.
Marriages fall apart.
Sickness pervades.
Pain prevails.
Loved ones leave us.
We grieve over death.
Justice disappears.
The righteous are imprisoned.
Leaders are corrupt.
Poverty strikes the powerless.
War breaks out.
The storms grow stronger.

As the rain falls, Lord,
Give us the courage to call out Your name.
Give us voices that can sing Your praises.
Give us energy to dance for You.
For You are a God who is faithful to us.
Your righteousness prevails.
You are loyal in Your promises,
And Your love is ever-flowing.

Let us praise our loving Father,
In rain, thunder, winds and lightning,
For these storms can never darken the light of God.
Amen.

Keeping Life in Rhythm

Lent 14

Everywhere one looks in nature, there are signs that God has a sense of rhythm.

As the moon moves through its various phases of light and darkness, the ocean responds to its gravitational pull on the earth, creating a rhythmic tide that moves into and away from the beach. Some say that a full moon even has effects upon human behavior.

Many trees participate in this rhythm as they clothe themselves in fresh green shoots before moving to the darker green foliage that will be their wardrobe for many months. Before completely unclothing themselves for the winter, they dazzle us with spectacular autumn colors before letting go of their leaves to fall to the earth.

The animals understand life's rhythm. Their courtship rituals are a result of an instinctive urge to reproduce that is triggered by the rhythm of nature. In the spring, the gobbler pumps himself up, drums the ground with his wing feathers, and spreads his tail feathers for an impressive display in hopes of attracting a hen.

In the fall, the whitetail buck secretes fluids from glands on his legs. As he moves through the forest, he leaves a scent on bushes and trees announcing that he is in the territory looking for a doe.

Each day has a rhythm for us as well. We wake up in the mornings about the same time, except for the millions that work at night, and go through much of the same routine as we prepare for the day. We go through the day following a schedule. Schedules keep us in rhythm, moving us from one appointment and task to another. About the same time each night, we lie down for sleep. Our bodies sense the change in pace. The beating of the heart slows, blood pressure drops, and breathing becomes regulated.

Rhythm is good. Most can testify to the difficulties placed upon body, mind and spirit when life throws us a change-up of circumstances that detrimentally interrupts the flow of day or night.

When our bodies are deprived of sleep or the sovereignty to control the pace of the day, rhythm is interrupted, and it's more difficult to function. The routines of life, once taken for granted, come to be longed for.

On the other hand, when there is never a change in the rhythm of life, when it stays the same day after day, month after month, and year after year, life can become boring. What would a musical score be without a change in rhythm? I suppose it would be a chant. That's useful in some settings, but it doesn't make for good music.

At least a chant is pleasant to the ears. Some people's lives have not only lost rhythm, but they have become arrhythmic, more akin to the beat that occurs when a three-year-old sits down and plays the piano. There is no longer any rhythm, only noise.

When people sit down with a counselor to discuss why their lives have fallen into disarray, the counselor's goal is to help people discover why they have lost touch with an internal beat of happiness and joy. The goal is to empower people to recognize a healthy rhythm and to reestablish it.

Unlike nature, whose rhythm is mostly controlled by a set of instincts and laws, we have been given great latitude in choosing the beat we will follow. If you find your life out of rhythm, perhaps it's time to allow God to become your metronome. I am not saying that when we end up in a wilderness of arrhythmic life that it is because we have lost our faith or that we have always wandered from God, but sometimes we have lost our way amidst the temptations that come our way or the great pressures placed upon us by living this challenging life.

But there is Good News! God is in the wilderness! While God may use many paths to bring our lives back in rhythm, ultimately, God, the Great Metronome, must be our source of healing. After all, God is the One who created rhythm. God did this in the beginning when He created day and night, six days of work and one day of rest—the rhythm of a week.

Most importantly, God created us in His image and placed us in a rhythmic world. His desire was for us to follow His beat, not the beat we set for ourselves.

Reading this book is an indication that you are seeking a rhythm that is right for your life. What are you hearing?

For a few years as a child, I took piano lessons from Mrs. Philpot. When I had problems following the timing of a piece of music, she would open the triangular wooden box and release a metal rod that was held back by tension. She then moved a little device on the rod that controlled the speed of its movement. "Tick, tick, tick, tick" went the metronome in a rhythm that dictated how fast or slow I was to play the piece of music.

When people become bored with the pace of life, they will often look for action in the world to spice it up. Sometimes this action is benign, but other times this action damages our relationships with our family, close friends, and to God. Caught in our sin, many times we will turn to unhealthy measures to escape the pain. We often look within ourselves and follow the beat of our own metronome, or we look outside of ourselves and follow the beat that is set by the world when our lives get out of rhythm. God wants us to allow Him to set the pace, like the conductor of a symphony.

God places within us His Spirit to move us. It is the movements of our lives that reflect our character and our distinctiveness. If God's Spirit is within us, we should have a desire to follow God's decrees and God's laws. But if God's Spirit is not within us, our hearts will be like hearts of stone. We will not yield to our Conductor. We will follow the beat that we determine, as opposed to the one God says is best for us.

Ezekiel once said to the Israelites:

I will sprinkle clean water on you, and you will be clean; I will cleanse you from all your impurities and from all your idols. I will give you a new heart and put a new spirit in you; I will remove from you your heart of stone and give you a heart of flesh. And I will put my Spirit in you and move you to follow my decrees and be careful to keep my laws. (Ezekiel. 36:25-27)

Inevitably, life will get out of rhythm. Sometimes it has to do with out-side forces that are beyond our control. But even then, we still control how we will respond. Then there are other times that the rhythm of life is lost because we have not followed the decrees and laws of God; God has ceased to be our Conductor. When He stops setting the metronome in our lives, we will end up in a wilderness.

What we need is to hear the words of Ezekiel. We need to receive the Lord's renewing Spirit and be cleansed from our impurities and re-moved from our idols. Then we can be assured of having the rhythm of a heart that is set to the Lord's metronome. It's as rejuvenating as the sights, sounds, and smells of a beautiful spring morning, as nature follows the rhythm God laid out from the beginning of time.

Prayer

God of Perfect Timing,

Like a brilliant composer, You have set a pattern and tempo for our lives. In waking and sleeping, in working and resting, in planting and harvesting, You teach us that there is a time for every season under Your good purpose.

Lord, though we don't always understand Your timing, You have assured us that You have a great plan for all creation. You have written our names on the palm of Your hand, and You will not forget us in Your magnificent redemption.

Teach us patience so we can faithfully follow the path You set before us. Help us to pace ourselves on our journey, so we do not rush through life and take it for granted. Allow us rest when we are weary. Give us energy when we need to move forward. Encourage us when we need to change our ways.

Holy God, may we always follow Your rhythm, dancing and singing for You alone in the mysterious symphony of our lives.

Amen.

Speak to a Stranger During Lent

Lent 15

Adults teach children not to speak to strangers for their own safety. Even though I'm not bound by this rule as an adult, I often follow it, not because I'm afraid of people I don't know, but because it takes energy for me to get involved in a lengthy discussion with a stranger.

There are some people who are energized by having conversations with others. These people, sometimes referred to as extroverts, can carry on a lengthy conversation with almost anyone and enjoy it. Other people are energized by spending time alone. It's sometimes difficult to get a grunt out of an extreme introvert.

I tend to be extroverted around people I know; introverted around people I don't know. I give a lot of myself to others in my job. So when I'm away from my work, I usually become introverted. My batteries need recharging, I suppose. Even though there is nothing wrong with this, I miss opportunities for ministry, especially with strangers, as I learned when our family took a vacation to Washington, D.C. when our sons were young.

The waiter, who seated us each morning for breakfast at a Holiday Inn in Washington, was a stranger, of course. His accent hinted that he was not American, certainly not unusual in the nation's capital. The accent sounded familiar to our family, and by the second day our elder son, twelve-years-old at the time, realized he had heard that accent before.

Our son John never meets a stranger. For example, at stops at McDonald's he might call the person behind the register by her name. "Hi Jennifer," he'd say, reading her name tag as if he knew her personally.

He conversed with a little girl at the airport shuttle as they compared scrape marks on their arms. Adults looked on, admiring the freedom as the two talked, uninhibited by social barriers.

It did not surprise me when John asked the waiter at our hotel breakfast if he was from Liberia. At the time, my wife and I, with the help of other friends, were sponsoring a Liberian student in college. He stayed with us between semesters, so John was familiar with his distinct accent. "Yes, I am from Liberia," the man responded with surprise. "How did you know?" "My Dad has a friend from Liberia who stays with us sometimes," John said.

By this time, I had been pulled into the conversation. While our breakfast got cold, I became acquainted with a Liberian and the other employees of the restaurant. One was named Steve, a Catholic, I discovered. The other two employees, one male and one female, were Buddhist and Muslim, respectively, information they offered once they discovered I was a pastor. That's when the conversation quickly shifted to spiritual issues. I didn't carry the conversation in that direction, they did. They each respected my position as a Christian pastor and requested prayer for needs in their lives.

As I returned to eat my cold breakfast, I was stunned at how easily a child had led me into conversation with these people and how each one was receptive to my pastoral calling. It made me wonder how many other opportunities for ministry I miss because I don't give more of my time to conversing with strangers.

When it came time to pay our bill, our waiter said, "Don't worry about your bill, sir. Steve has paid for your breakfast this morning." Imagine that. My bill was paid by a total stranger, grateful for ten minutes of conversation. I thanked him as I left, and he simply said, "Pray for me pastor."

So that day I prayed for Steve and his friends, and I've tried to remember the lesson my son John taught me: it's okay to speak to strangers. After all, I believe Jesus did that on a number of occasions, like the time He initiated a conversation with a Samaritan woman at a well in Samaria. It was taboo for Him to speak to her because she was a woman and because she was a Samaritan, but Jesus broke tradition to minister to her.

If we always choose to remain in our world, how will those who don't know Jesus have the opportunity to be introduced to Him? There is a way to share Jesus without being obnoxious, over-bearing, or rude. It is true that we can share Jesus without saying a word. But it is also true that many times, words are required, and we must at least begin the conversation.

Every conversation doesn't lead to Jesus. Most often, relationships need to be established and trust must be earned before people will be receptive to a spiritual conversation. But sometimes, the door is opened quickly, just as it was in that restaurant in Washington, D.C.

During this season of Lent, keep in mind that there are many people walking in a wilderness. They are doing so quietly, alone, and they have no spiritual guidance or help. No one is praying for them or is showing any concern for their problems. They might welcome prayer from you, a total stranger. It's surprising what total strangers will share with those with empathetic ears. If you will take the time to listen and show sincere interest in a stranger, you might make a friend. You might have an opportunity to share with them the love of Christ and show them the way out of the wilderness. Not only will you have made a friend, but you also may begin a relationship where you will become a spiritual friend to this person for life.

And how can they preach unless they are sent? As it is written, "How beautiful are the feet of those who bring good news!" (Romans 10:15). If we sling Good News out, even to those we don't know, we never know when some seeds will land on fertile ground. That's a great way to get rid of a wilderness.

Prayer

Lord, you are no stranger to us. You broke into our world, interrupting our lives, so that we might know love. You boldly offered Your friendship to the friendless. You started conversations with people who didn't know You. You shared meals with those You had just met. You invited Yourself over to sinners' homes. You employed no-names to be Your disciples. You welcomed children. You went out of Your way to reach people.

Oh, that we might be so bold! Jesus, teach us Your ways. The strangers around us still need You in their lives. Bend our hearts toward the nameless faces we encounter each day. Put smiles on our faces as we pass by them in the grocery store. Give us kind words with which to greet them. Help us to listen to responses after we ask people, "How are You?" Let us show Your compassion, acceptance and concern to those we have yet to know.

You, Lord, have been no stranger to the world. May we proceed as lovingly and vulnerably in this life.

Amen.

Don't Leave the Gate of Your Character Unguarded

Lent 16

In August 2003, two ex-Georgia Tech football coaches were supposed to lead their football teams against one another in the Kickoff Classic at Giants' Stadium in East Rutherford, New Jersey: Ralph Friedgen with his Maryland Terrapins and George O'Leary as the new coach of the Notre Dame Fighting Irish.

It would have been O'Leary's second straight Kickoff Classic. In 2001 O'Leary coached his Georgia Tech Yellow Jackets to a 13-7 win over the Syracuse Orangemen. However, O'Leary never made it to the sidelines of Notre Dame, resigning only days after being hired as their head coach.

The record books will have to place an asterisk by O'Leary's name because there was incorrect information found on his coaching resume that called his integrity into question.

O'Leary's incident is a reminder to us all that we can build a great career and a great reputation only to have it dashed in a few days.

Don Johnson wrote, "In ancient China, the people desired security from the barbaric hordes to the north, so they built the Great Wall of China. It was so high they knew no one could climb over it and so thick that nothing could break it down. They settled back to enjoy their security. During the first hundred years of the wall's existence, China was invaded three times. Not once did the barbaric hordes break down the wall or climb over the top. Each time they bribed a gatekeeper and then marched right through the gate. The Chinese were so busy relying on the walls of stone that they forgot to teach integrity to the children who grew up to guard the gates."[21]

It's a great temptation for successful people to rely on great achievements as their security. Regardless of the level of their achievement, if people have lapses of integrity, the gate of their reputation is left unguarded, jeopardizing their ability to lead. O'Leary's incident teaches that lapses of integrity, even from years ago, can have devastating consequences on a person's future and his or her ability to lead.

"Integrity" comes from a Latin root that carries with it a sense of wholeness. The wall of China has integrity because it is solid. Likewise, a person with integrity is solid in ethics and judgment. A person with integrity discerns right from wrong and acts on it, unafraid to state why a particular position was taken. Integrity takes courage because sometimes being a person of integrity comes with a personal cost. However, the cost of leaving the gates of your moral code or ethics unguarded is much higher.

In the Bible we see many examples of the cost of having a lapse of integrity. The book of 2 Samuel says that "in the spring, at the time when kings go off to war...David remained in Jerusalem" (11:1). The implication is that David should have been at war with his men, but instead he remained at his palace.

There was no place where David was safer than in the well-fortified surroundings of the palace. Yet it was from the roof of the palace that David saw a beautiful woman bathing, and he sent someone to find out about her. The gates to the palace were well guarded, but David left the gate of his moral code of ethics unguarded. One bad decision led to another.

Later when news came that the woman was pregnant, David had her husband brought home from the battlefield believing he would sleep with his wife, which would later cause him to believe the child was his own. But Uriah was a man of such integrity that he slept at the entrance to the palace with all his master's servants and did not go down to his house. He refused to have pleasure with his wife because of his loyalty to the men he left behind, who were camped in the open fields. Uriah's integrity cost him his life. King David had him sent to the front lines where he was killed.

David suffered too, as did Bathsheba. God's prophet Nathan foretold the death of their child who was to be born. Though David pleaded with God to spare the child, the child did not live.

Even with these terrible lapses of judgment in David's life, he is still lifted up as the greatest King of Israel. David provides an example that a few bad decisions should not sum up the character of one's life. In fact, in speaking to King Solomon about David, God said,

> As for you, if you walk before me in integrity of heart and uprightness, as David your father did, and do all I command and observe my decrees and laws, I will establish your royal throne over Israel forever, as I promised David your father when I said, "You shall never fail to have a man on the throne of Israel." (1 Kings 9:4-5)

In spite of the lack of integrity David exhibited by not being with his soldiers on the battlefield, in having the affair with Bathsheba, in trying to cover it up by bringing Uriah home, and then, by sending him to the front lines to his death, these incidents did not sum up the character of King David over the course of his life.

Likewise, the falsifying of his resume years ago does not sum up the character of George O'Leary. I base this on the way he handled his resignation, by the reputation he has in coaching, and by the productive years of coaching he has had since 2003. He was honest, forthright, gracious, and repentant. He explained how as a young married father he had allowed his pursuit of the dream to be a football coach to cloud his judgment in preparing his resume, which in later years was never corrected.

In his resignation remarks, O'Leary said, "I pray that my experiences will simply be yet another coaching lesson to the youth of this country that we are all accountable for our actions and there can be no double standard."[22]

He is right. If we think otherwise, we've left the gate to our character unguarded.

The season of Lent is a good time to take inventory of our character. Are we harboring anything in our closets that would be damaging to our reputation? Are we tempted to cut corners and shave the edges in order to get ahead? Even if we should see our reputation as being beyond reproach, shouldn't we be careful that pride doesn't become the measuring rod of our character?

Remember, a wilderness is only a day or two away for any of us should we sacrifice our integrity on the altar of success, fame, or popularity. While O'Leary may be the poster child for that lesson, he has also modeled that the wilderness doesn't have to be a final destination; it can be a temporary place for those who acknowledge their mistakes, learn from them, and seek to move on with a redeemed and successful journey. While the world doesn't always offer that chance, that's the business in which God specializes.

Prayer

Righteous God,

Our culture worships many things: celebrity, wealth, heroism, intelligence and power. Yet rarely does it lift up the value of integrity. Like David, we have been guilty of making poor decisions. We have blatantly chosen wrong paths because they looked attractive or seemed easier.

Lord, these paths have only led us straight into the wilderness where it becomes more and more difficult to hear Your voice.

Call out to us, Great God, when we are lost in the shadows of our sin. Let us hear Your perfect Word; teach us of our wrongdoing, as Nathan taught David. Give us the courage to confess our awfulness before You and others whom we have hurt. Have mercy on us!

Create in us clean hearts, and renew our spirits. Carry us back to the place of righteousness. Help us to live a life of truth, integrity and humility so we can experience the joy of Your saving grace once more.

Amen.

Thanking Those
Who Touch Our Lives
Lent 17

"Samuel Leibowitz, a criminal lawyer, saved 78 people from the electric chair. Not one ever thanked him. Art King helped 2,500 people find jobs through his radio program, "Job Center of the Air." Only ten ever thanked him. One year, an official of the post office in charge of the dead letter box in Washington, D.C., stated that the address received hundreds of thousands of letters addressed to Santa Claus, but only one letter came thanking Santa for the gifts he brought."[23] Jesus once healed ten men with leprosy. Only one returned to give thanks.

Anyone stand guilty? I should be more thankful to my parents for all they've done for me. I should thank my wife more for what she does for our family. We take her for granted too often. We just expect her to fill the roles she has always filled in our home.

My church has provided me with a wonderful opportunity to fulfill my calling to ministry, but I don't express my thanks enough. Are you as guilty as I?

Our City Council, County Commissioners, and Board of Education work on our behalf to keep our city, county, and school systems strong, but rarely do we thank them for their work.

Our police officers, fire fighters, and paramedics fulfill very important functions. Many of them are volunteers. We expect them to be there when we call, well trained and ready for any emergency. I'm sure they could use a sincere "thank you" from us for their sacrifices.

Our soldiers leave their families behind and place their lives in harm's way in order to defend the freedoms represented by Old Glory. Can we ever thank them enough? Veteran's Day comes and goes each year with many people never saying "thank you" to a veteran.

Our school teachers take our children who are sometimes un-ruly and disrespectful and try to inspire them to achieve their best through the pursuit of an education. Where would our society be with-out their dedication?

A postal worker told me that she once received a letter of thanks from a woman on her mail route, the only one she's ever received. Since delivering the mail is her job, most people take her hard work for grant-ed, which is why that one letter meant enough to her that she had it framed.

Chris Smith, who writes for an online church bulletin, tells about a famous minister and teacher who suffered from depression. William L. Stidger, mired in a fog of depression, was given the suggestion by a friend to think of people who had benefited him in his life. His friend told him to ask himself whether he had ever thanked any of these people. Stidger's quick reply was that he could not recall ever thanking any of them. His friend suggested that he write these people some personal letters of thanks.[24]

Stidger had a love for literature, and he traced that love back to a teacher named Miss Smith. After writing her and thanking her for the influence she had in his life, he received a letter in a shaky handwriting: "Dear Willy, I remembered you as a little fellow in my class. You have warmed my old heart. I have taught school for fifty years. Yours is the first letter of thanks I ever received from a student, and I shall cherish it until I die" (Smith).

According to Smith, "This response so encouraged Stidger that he wrote another letter and another. After five hundred letters, he stopped. He was no longer downcast. All of us have benefited from a host of people—parents, teachers, schoolmates, friends, preachers, fel-low Christians. Are you in the dumps, feeling sorry for yourself? Pick up a pen and write a letter. Go dial the number of a friend. Express thanks!" (Smith).

To the Samaritan who returned to thank Jesus for His healing, Jesus asked, "Were not all ten cleansed? Where are the other nine?" (Luke 17:17).

It's easy for us to be in the same category as the nine cleansed leapers who were healed but who did not return to give thanks. Each one had places to go, things to do, people to see. No doubt all of them were thankful. They had all been in a wilderness for a long time. They had been cast out of society. They were not allowed to have physical contact with other people. They were rejected by friends and family. The priest said they were unclean. As soon as they were healed, their heads must have simply overrun their hearts.

But what excuse does that leave us? If we would simply turn off the television for one night, we could find time to thank a few people we've never thanked before. If we would use the Internet constructively for a few hours, we could touch people we've not touched in years with words that have power. This would be a good discipline for us during Lent. This is a good time to count our blessings and to bless those who have made opportunities possible for us.

You never know how a simple "thank-you" might change some-one's life. It might even be your own. Words of thanks have the power to make hope, joy, happiness, and love bloom in the wilderness.

Prayer

Lord, sometimes it is so difficult for us to stop for a few moments in our day and show appreciation to those who have dedicated their lives to service. All too often we gladly accept the help of others without even acknowledging their sacrifices. We do this to others, and we do this to You, God. So today we offer You a prayer of thanksgiving for You and all Your earthly angels who serve this world so diligently. Help us to remember those who serve so thanklessly in this world, and give us the wisdom to show our appreciation to them.

For those who ensure public safety:
> Police officers,
> Military personnel,
> Government officials,
> Fire fighters,
> Security guards,

Lord, we give You thanks and ask for Your blessing on their lives.

For those who care for us in times of sickness and death:
> Doctors and nurses,
> Hospice workers,
> Mental health professionals,
> Elderly caregivers,
> Paramedics,

Lord, we give You thanks and ask for Your blessing on their lives.

For those who devote their work to children:
> Educators,
> Coaches,
> Daycare workers,
> Community Center leaders,
> Parents and grandparents,

Lord, we give You thanks and ask for Your blessing on their lives.

For those who volunteer their time to help others:
> Habitat for Humanity workers,
> Soup kitchen chefs,
> Peace Corps personnel,
> Food Bank operators,
> And all other non-profits,
Lord, we give You thanks and ask for Your blessing on their lives.

For those who serve God's creation:
> Veterinarians,
> Animal rescuers,
> Environmentalists,
> Gardeners,
Lord, we give You thanks and ask for Your blessing on their lives.

Amen.

Who Is Your Navigator?
Lent 18

I have a decent sense of direction. So far I've made it back from every place I've been. I can't say that I've always made it to every place I've started out for, though. Although I am a male, I have overcome the Moses syndrome: I no longer wander around in the wilderness without asking for directions.

There is one major exception. When my wife rides shotgun, I can't find my way out of a paper bag. Since I usually do well on my own, it seems that this problem must be her fault. She says to me after I've started out in a wrong direction for a well-known location, "I don't know how you ever get anywhere without me."

This is part of the problem. I have been conditioned by 27 years of marriage that when she's in the car with me I am supposed to rely on her for help. I know I'm going to get instructions whether I need them or not. Subconsciously, I think I actually start out in a wrong direction just to reassure her that she's needed.

I suppose I must take the blame for all of this. In the beginning of this relationship, it seemed easier for us to divide up trips with me as the driver and her as the navigator. I drove while she looked at the map and gave me directions. That way I could never be blamed for getting us lost, not logically anyway.

However, somewhere along the way, she started taking privilege with this navigational role. She navigated even when I didn't need a navigator. If I protested, she'd respond that she *didn't* know I didn't need a navigator and that she was *just* trying to help.

For example, there are those times when we run errands across town. Surely she knows that I know how to get across town. Since there's usually more than one way across town, I inevitably choose a route different from the one she would have chosen. So it doesn't take long before we have a conversation like this: "Where are you going?" she asks. "I'm going to the market," I respond. "Well, why are you going this way?" she asks. Before I can defend my answer, I am told that I'm taking the long route, which is a waste of time and gas and money.

After many years of this, I am now conditioned not to think about directions at all when my wife is in the car. I just put my brain in neutral. She would contend it was there already. I just drive and wait for directions.

Many people live their lives this way. They don't think much about the direction their lives are taking. Their lives are like leaves that land in a stream; they go wherever the flow of life takes them. They seem to have no directional impetus of their own. They go where they are told. They may be behind the wheel directing their own lives, but they are so heavily influenced by others that they do not exercise any autonomy.

If the peer group says "turn here to be popular," they turn. If the advertising agency tells them to buy a product to be cool, they buy it. If a boyfriend says, "You must be intimate with me to show me your love," she does. If the pressure mounts to keep up with the neighbors in affluence, the couple spends more than they can afford.

In addition, the world is filled with people who move through life with no sense of direction for this life or for the one to come. When every thought is tied to temporal matters, to the earth and all it contains, people will eventually come to a day of crisis when they realize that the direction their lives are heading is uncertain and the future is unclear.

The Bible tells us that this day of crisis will be extended to a great Day of Judgment when God will gather all the nations and judge the people, separating them as a shepherd would separate sheep from goats.

Life doesn't have to be lived in fear of judgment. Life can be lived with peace and assurance. Though we do not know the future, we can know the One who holds the future. Though we cannot know the bends the road ahead of us will take, we can proceed with confidence that regardless of where life leads, the Holy Spirit, our life's Navigator, is present as our guide.

The following is a popular story found on various Internet sites. The story goes like this:

In January 2000, leaders in Charlotte, North Carolina, invited their favorite son, Billy Graham, to a luncheon in his honor. Rev. Graham initially hesitated to accept the invitation because of his struggles with Parkinson's disease. But the Charlotte leaders said, "We don't expect a major address. Just come and let us honor you." So he agreed.[25]

After wonderful things were said about him, Rev. Graham stepped to the rostrum, looked at the crowd, and said, "I'm reminded today of Albert Einstein, the great physicist who this month has been honored by *Time* magazine as the Man of the Century. Einstein was once traveling from Princeton on a train when the conductor came down the aisle, punching the tickets of every passenger. When he came to Einstein, Einstein reached in his vest pocket. He couldn't find his ticket, so he reached in his other pocket. It wasn't there, so he looked in his briefcase but couldn't find it. Then he looked in the seat by him. He couldn't find it" (Wimer).

"The conductor said, 'Dr. Einstein, I know who you are. We all know who you are. I'm sure you bought a ticket. Don't worry about it.' Einstein nodded appreciatively. The conductor continued down the aisle punching tickets. As he was ready to move to the next car, he turned around and saw the great physicist down on his hands and knees looking under his seat for his ticket" (Wimer).

"The conductor rushed back and said, 'Dr. Einstein, Dr. Einstein, don't worry, I know who you are. No problem. You don't need a ticket. I'm sure you bought one.' Einstein looked at him and said, 'Young man, I too, know who I am. What I don't know is where I'm going'" (Wimer).

Having said that Billy Graham continued, "See the suit I'm wearing? It's a brand-new suit. My wife, my children, and my grandchildren are telling me I've gotten a little slovenly in my old age. I used to be a bit more fastidious. So I went out and bought a new suit for this luncheon and one more occasion" (Wimer).

"You know what that occasion is? This is the suit in which I'll be buried. But when you hear I'm dead, I don't want you to immediately remember the suit I'm wearing. I want you to remember this: I not only know who I am. I also know where I'm going" (Wimer).

The Bible is written so that each of us might have the assurance of where we are going. Since none of us have ever been to heaven, it stands to reason that we must all get directions to go there. When we ask for directions, the Lord says, "I'll do you one better. I'll take you there. Take up your cross and follow me."

Heaven is a place that Jesus has prepared for His disciples. The Lord has shown us that the road to heaven begins right here on earth. When the Lord comes into our hearts and washes away our sins, the Holy Spirit becomes our navigator and sets us on the narrow road.

One of our major problems after committing our lives to the Lord is that we like to take back the navigational decision-making from Him. Don't you remember? Jesus said, "Take up [your] cross and FOLLOW me" (Luke 9:23, emphasis added). Being a disciple of Jesus is about being a follower.

Any attempt to take back the navigational rights to our lives will put us in the wilderness. We may live for some time thinking we are making great choices. Eventually, we will top a hill, and we will discover nothing before us but a vast wilderness. We will wonder what went wrong. We will try to retrace our steps and figure out what decision we made that could have been made differently. We can always trace it back to the point where we laid down our cross and stopped following Jesus. "There is a path before each person that seems right, but it ends in death" (Proverbs 14:12, NLT).

What navigational choices are you currently withholding from God? Are you withholding choices about your finances? Are you spending time in places that are unhealthy for you? Are you allowing others to navigate your life by influencing decisions you are making? Are you going to places on the Internet that are addicting and unholy?

Are your navigational decisions landing you in a wilderness? The Children of Israel lived in a wilderness for forty years because they would not allow God to lead them through Moses into the Promised Land. God wanted to give it to them, but they didn't have the faith to claim it. It just didn't seem right because the people there were bigger and stronger. They were afraid, even though they had witnessed God's mighty hand save them from the Egyptians.

Are you confident in your navigational decision making? Don't be. Allow Jesus to be the navigator. He knows the way through this world. More importantly, He knows the way to heaven.

Prayer

Brilliant Lord,

In our wilderness wandering, we easily forget that You are the light who leads our paths. Instead of following Your guidance, we seek out other ways to follow. We look for security on the paths of success, money, addiction, and entertainment, but all too soon we realize we have gotten ourselves more lost in the darkness of the wilderness. And we can't help but feel that we are going nowhere.

Jesus, You are our only way out! It is Your compassion, Your courage, Your forgiveness, Your wisdom, and Your love that can lift us out of the darkness and take us back to the lighted path of God. Help us, Messiah. We need Your redemption. Be our leader and our guide. Amen.

Making Room
for Others

Lent 19

It's getting crowded on Mother Earth. In 1970 there were less than four billion people living on the planet. In 1986 we went over the five billion mark. In 1999 we passed the six billion mark. In October 2011, we exceeded seven billion people on planet earth. We added another billion in just a little more than ten years.[26]

In a world that is getting increasingly crowded and in a place where resources are becoming less plentiful, we are becoming increasingly concerned about keeping much for ourselves, and less concerned about whether others have any for themselves.

Even though the biblical world had plenty of space, resources were still scarce. People have always struggled with what to keep and what to share. In the book of Acts, Lydia opened her heart to Paul's message about the love of Jesus and was baptized along with her family. Afterward, she opened up her home to Paul and Luke.

Luke says, "She prevailed upon us" (Acts 16:15, NASB). In other words, she wouldn't take no for an answer. She made room for these strangers in her home, the very meaning of hospitality.

After God gave Moses the Ten Commandments and the Israelites were about to enter and possess the Promised Land, God told Moses that the people were to defend "the cause of the fatherless and the widow, and [love] the alien, giving him food and clothing. And you are to love those who are aliens, for you yourselves were aliens in Egypt" (Deuteronomy 10:18-19).

Because these people Moses was leading were once slaves

in Egypt, they, of all people, should have known what it was like to be strangers in a foreign land. Since they knew what it was like to be strangers and to wander in a wilderness, God instructed them through Moses to love these people in need.

Love here doesn't necessarily mean they should have an emotional connection to them, as much as it means to act in a loving way-giving these people food and clothing and shelter, to help care for their needs.

The love of strangers is not about placing us in unsafe and compromising situations. It is more about being inconvenienced for the benefit of others.

We often think that hospitality is a gift possessed only by women who can set a fine table, or create an environment where a home feels comfortable to anyone who visits. But anyone can play the role of host and use a variety of gifts to make room for others.

The more room we make for strangers and the more often we make room for them, the better we become at doing it. We soon learn that if we open up our homes, they don't have to look like those in *Better Homes and Gardens*.

What strangers or others care about is that we make an effort to make room for them for just a short period of time, that we open up our homes, our evenings, our hearts, our conversation to focus just on them. There are over seven billion people in this world, so when we make room for a stranger or a friend, it means something (Levine).

Rev. Bill Versteeg tells the story of the time he and his wife were students at Dordt College. They were returning to the school when their Volkswagen van broke down in Moose Jaw, Saskatchewan in January. They managed to get the Volkswagen going again, but the trip to the next town that usually took less than an hour took four. They had no heat and were traveling in 35 below zero temperatures.[27]

They telephoned the pastor of the Christian Reformed Church in Regina. His name was Rev. Peter Plug. He led them to his house, fed them a warm meal, gave them a place to sleep, and called a man in the church who came over and picked up their van. The mechanic pulled the engine, repaired it, and put them back on the road the next day. That family never forgot the gifts of hospitality and service. When you make room for others in your lives, they know that you love them and they know you care. Christians should be known as people who make room in our lives for others because that's the nature of the God we worship (Versteeg).

Perhaps this is why the Apostle Peter wrote: "Offer hospitality to one another without grumbling. Each one should use whatever gift he has received to serve others, faithfully administering God's grace in its various forms" (1 Peter 4:9-10).

It's easy to be hospitable to those we enjoy being around and to those who might return the favor. However, we grumble when we are asked to be hospitable to those who are not so easy to love, whose reputation might not help ours, when it interrupts our plans, and when it costs us something.

But I remind you that over 2000 years ago, Joseph knocked on an innkeeper's door in Bethlehem and was turned away. "No room."

So the Savior was born in a cattle stable. Had the innkeeper known that Mary was carrying the Messiah, would he have found a better place for her to give birth?

The writer of Hebrews says, "Do not forget to entertain strangers, for by so doing some people have entertained angels without knowing it" (Hebrews 13:2).

Thus, in the process of making room for others, the sacrifice will bring its own share of rewards and blessings. The cost of keeping all of our space for ourselves means that we will simply fill it up with things of this world that will pass away and leave us wandering in a spiritual wilderness.

During this season of Lent, will you reach out to one person or family and open up your home to them?

If you don't like bringing people into your home, can you think of one way you can open your life to other people, both to those you know and to those you don't?

How can you allow others to interrupt your life in a way that you can show them the love of Jesus?

Look, our lives aren't perfect, and they don't have to be in order to make room for others. If you wait until you have everything together, you will never make room for others.

I read recently that one mom opened up her home to the Parent

Teacher Association. All of them marveled at her clean home. She said, "Thank God they didn't look too closely. I'd put all the dirty dishes in the oven and stuffed the overflowing piles of dirty clothes and the stinky dog bed in the hall closet."[28]

If you wait until you've got it all together to make room for others, you will never make room for anyone.

But one thing we learn from the scriptures is that Lydia chose to make room for Paul and Luke after she received the gospel and was baptized.

That seems to be the difference maker for Christians: the presence of Jesus. The presence of Jesus calls us to make room for others because Jesus has made room for us through His love and His grace. And there's still plenty of room for anyone, like Lydia, who would come and accept Christ and agree to be baptized as a sign of faith in Him.

Prayer

There are strangers among us,
In our neighborhoods,
In our churches,
Even in our families.

There are strangers among us,
Across county lines,
Across state borders,
Across oceans and continents.

There are strangers among us,
Who have been banished to the wilderness.
They are the homeless.
They are the mentally ill.
They are the hungry.
They are the downcast.
They are the refugees.
They are the imprisoned.
They are the exploited.
They are the lonely.
They are the lost.

While there are strangers among us, Jesus,
You never had strangers around You.
Everyone You met, You called
Friend.
Sister.
Brother.
Child.
Beloved.

You always made room in Your heart for wanderers.
And You invited them
To eat and drink with You,
To follow You,
To tell You about their problems,
To be Your disciples.

Let us love strangers as You did, Christ.
With Your compassion,
With Your hospitality,
With Your patience,
With Your grace,
With Your heart.
Let us, like You, welcome wandering angels to walk beside us on our journey Home.
Amen.

God Used Rosa Parks to Help Us Change Our Ways

Lent 20

He lived by what He taught. When the Romans came for Him and beat Him incessantly, He could have called ten thousand angels to His defense. Instead, He turned the other cheek. After they nailed Him to the cross, mocked Him, demeaned Him publicly in the most shameful way possible, He still prayed for them, asking God to forgive them for their sins. Upon seeing how Jesus died, the centurion said from the foot of the cross, "Surely this was a righteous man" (Luke 23:47).

A few years ago, someone asked me a piercing question about the Sermon of the Plains (or the Sermon on the Mount from Matthew's Gospel): "Where is the line between turning the other cheek and being someone's doormat?" Wow! What a great question! "Jesus. Oh, Jesus. I need you to come answer this lady's question for me, please."

Jesus let me struggle with that question for a while. Later that day, when I heard that Rosa Parks, the mother of the civil rights movement, had died at the age of 92, I felt as if I'd found part of the answer to her question.

Rosa Parks was tired of being a doormat, and she was tired of her people being doormats. It was a simple request, but in politely refusing to give up her seat on the bus, Rosa Parks drew a line in the sand. Through her defiance, a movement was started which we embrace today as the catalyst of the Civil Rights Movement. But, how was Rosa's action Christ-like? How did her actions measure up against the words of Jesus as taught in the passage previously mentioned?

Jesus said in His sermon: "Give to everyone who asks you, and if anyone takes what belongs to you, do not demand it back" (Luke 6:30).

If you interpret Jesus' words literally, Rosa Parks didn't do what Jesus said to do. The white man asked the black seamstress for her seat on the bus. Wasn't she obliged to give it up? If not on the basis of the South's culture of racial separation of the day, which demanded that she do so, how about as a follower of Jesus? Didn't Jesus say "Give to everyone who asks"?

We cannot take everything that Jesus said to its literal extremes. Jesus once said:

> If your hand or your foot causes you to sin, cut it off and throw it away. It is better for you to enter life maimed or crippled than to have two hands or two feet and be thrown into eternal fire. And if your eye causes you to sin, gouge it out and throw it away. It is better for you to enter life with one eye than to have two eyes and be thrown into the fire of hell. (Matt. 18:8-9)

People in their right minds would never actually cut off parts of their bodies in order to fulfill this commandment of Jesus. Jesus would never want that. What's the intent of His message? Sometimes we must go to extreme measures in order to keep sin out of our lives. That's the message!

When we interpret Jesus' message in the statement, "Give to everyone who asks you, and if anyone takes what belongs to you, do not demand it back," we must use the same logic. What if we gave to everyone who asks? Wouldn't that be psychotic? What if someone asked for sex? What if someone asked us for our entire paycheck? What if someone asked for our child? You might say that these are ridiculous scenarios. Perhaps. They are intended to show that Jesus' words have a general intent and should not be taken to a literal extreme.

The general intent of His words about our enemies is that we must seek to change our enemies by loving them. Perhaps in loving them we can actually make them our friends. By our love we can show them the error of their ways. We can make some enemies into friends by showing kindness to them; by surprising them with non-violent behavior and unbelievable generosity. In short, we should act lovingly toward them. This doesn't guarantee that they will cease being our enemies. In fact,

Jesus' enemies didn't cease being His. Instead, they killed Him. Likewise, many African Americans died in non-violent protests seeking a change in the laws of our country.

Rosa Parks' actions were non-violent. Non-violent resistance became the cornerstone of the Civil Rights Movement under the leadership of Dr. Martin Luther King, Jr. Rosa Parks' resistance was in keeping with the spirit of what Jesus taught in this passage, as she sought to overcome evil with good, although she didn't follow what He taught in a literal sense.

Jesus also demonstrated in His life that there are times when the enemy must be confronted directly with his evil ways. Evil must be resisted or else it will continue. Evil can be resisted even while we are still loving those who are perpetrating the evil. The truth of the Civil Rights Movement is that without the non-violent resistance to the racial inequalities of our laws, change might have never occurred.

While Rosa Parks wasn't the first brave soul to emerge in defiance of unjust laws, she was the first to be cast into the spotlight, and the one for whom the torch of the Civil Rights Movement would be carried for future generations because of her courage not to move.

In defying the order to move from her seat on that bus in Montgomery, she wasn't only making a "stand" for herself; she represented all African Americans who continued to be subjected to that kind of injustice. In that sense, her refusal to move was a way of loving others who continued to be demeaned as she was being demeaned.

Her actions remind me of those of the Apostle Paul and Silas. While preaching in Philippi they were arrested, beaten, and thrown into prison. After an earthquake shook the prison, causing the cells of the prison doors to come open and the chains of the prisoners to break free from the walls, they didn't escape. Instead they witnessed to the jailer and convinced him to become a believer in Jesus.

> *When it was daylight, the magistrates sent their officers*
> *to the jailer with the order: "Release those men." The jailer*
> *told Paul, "The magistrates have ordered that you and*
> *Silas be released. Now you can leave. Go in peace." But*
> *Paul said to the officers: "They beat us publicly without*

a trial, even though we are Roman citizens, and threw us
into prison. And now do they want to get rid of us quietly?
No! Let them come themselves and escort us out." (Acts
16:35-37)

Paul stood up for himself and against the injustice shown to him and his friend Silas. In doing so, he was standing up for all Roman citizens. Should this injustice go unchecked, what would prevent them from beating another Roman citizen?

Paul and Silas' protest was not contrary to the teachings and the nature of Jesus. By speaking out they were not allowing evil to go unchecked.

Of course the questions are raised, "What's evil? What's good? What must be done?" It's easy to draw the line in such a way as to put ourselves on the side of the good and others on the side of evil. Jesus warned us plainly, though, about making the mistake of the Pharisees by pointing out the speck in our brother's eye while having a log in our own. Should we get past that dilemma, evil ought to be easy enough to identify. It ought to be. But the Civil Rights Movement reminds us just how easy it is for us to have logs in our eyes. Thankfully, God sends us people like Rosa Parks who have helped us see ourselves as we really are simply by refusing to be a doormat any longer.

There's still more to be done. What work have you contributed to race relations? Have you the courage to draw the line where evil is being done?

Do you have the courage to stand up when there is prejudice being levied against the poor, the overweight, the wealthy, the politically liberal or conservative, women, homosexuals, the elderly, immigrants, believers of other religions? Prejudice comes in a variety of forms. Where is your weakness?

I realize some of you reacted negatively to some of the categories in the above list. However, we don't have to agree with people's choices before we stand against those who are mistreating them. Jesus stood with the woman caught in adultery, before she turned from her sin. He stood against the prejudices of those who were rallying against her. Not only must we do that to be like Jesus, but in order to be forgiven by Jesus we must confess when we are among those with rocks in our hands seeking to harm someone instead of love them.

May we continue to strive to fulfill the words of our Declaration of Independence, which states that "all men [people] are created equal, that they are endowed by their Creator with certain unalienable Rights, that among these are Life, Liberty and the pursuit of Happiness."

Just having these words in a document doesn't make them so. Otherwise, the Civil Rights Movement would never have been necessary, and slavery would never have been a part of our history. Otherwise, the Women's Suffrage Movement would not have been necessary. Otherwise, the law preventing poor whites who could not afford to own land from voting would not have had to be changed. We must live to make sure the words of the Declaration remain a reality for ALL people, even though those words obviously did not mean "all people" in its original intent.

Just because our African-American brothers and sisters moved through that wilderness and in some ways have found the Promised Land that Rev. Martin Luther King, Jr. dreamed about, that dream is far from a reality for many African Americans, other minorities, and even for many poor whites. Poverty is no respecter of persons. Hunger knows no color barrier.

During Lent, remember there is still injustice around us. God still calls people of all races and economic brackets to stand up for the powerless, to speak up for the defenseless, and to lift up the fallen. Yes, there may be a cost involved, but if you want some inspiration, look to the same person who inspired the leaders of our Civil Rights Movement; look to the One who went to the cross to stand up for all who were powerless over sin and defenseless over the enemy's temptations, and who was lifted up from the earth in order to draw all men and women to Himself. Look to Jesus.

Prayer

Creator of Perfect Justice,

Sometimes our greatest sins occur when we keep our mouths closed. We witness abuse, injustice and exploitation every day on our televisions, yet we passively sit on our couches and change the channel. You call us to confront the evil of the world, but we would rather distract ourselves from its unpleasantness.

Drag us out of our complacency, Almighty God! Force us to face injustice head on! Allow the evil in the world to shake us to our core! Re-sensitize us to the tragedy of violence, hunger, poverty and pain. Bring us to the edge of the wilderness, so we can see the truth of suffering.

Stir in us Your call to righteousness. Give us Your wisdom and courage to resist evil. Fortify our hearts to destroy evil with unabated love, compassion and peace. Open our eyes, ears, hands and hearts to Your people. Amen.

Oh, No!
Not Manna Again!
Lent 21

In a previous community where I lived, the local newspaper began a section called "Rant and Rave." People are allowed to call and leave a brief message, or to email a brief message to the paper stating their opinions on various subjects. After being screened, they are printed. No name is attached. No one takes ownership for the words of praise or complaint.

I never ran a scientific poll, but rants usually carried the day two or three to one. It's a part of our nature to complain, whether we take ownership for the complaint or not. I protested the style of journalism from the onset and I signed my name. I really felt the forum allowed venom to be spewed in a community and kept people stirred up with animosity toward one another. Others disagreed. "If I signed my name to a comment, I'd be fired," some would say. "This is a victory for the powerless to have a say without fear of retribution," another would write.In the end, the "Rant and Rave" section sold more papers and that won the day.

The Bible shows us that, at times, complaining can make matters worse, and at others, it serves a useful place in our faith. Consider Moses. Moses had to endure the complaints of the freed Hebrews as they traveled in the wilderness. The Bible says that for forty years the people ate manna.

I can eat turkey sandwiches for only about a week after Thanksgiving before I'm ready for something different, so I can't imagine eating the same food every day for 40 years. Had I been among those ancient Hebrews, it's likely I would have complained, just as they did.

Listen to their complaints from Numbers 11:4-6: "The rabble with them began to crave other food, and again the Israelites started wailing and said, 'If only we had meat to eat! We remember the fish we ate in Egypt at no cost—also the cucumbers, melons, leeks, onions and garlic. But now we have lost our appetite; we never see anything but this manna!'"

Of course, they could have gotten creative and took the lemons to lemonade approach and made manna hotcakes, manna waffles, manna burgers, manna bagels, topped off with a little bit of "bamanna" bread! They could have been thankful they were not starving. Instead they slid down Complainer's Hill. It's easy to do. One complaint usually leads to another.

The scripture says that the people complained to Moses and Moses complained to the Lord:

> *Why have you brought this trouble on your servant? What have I done to displease you that you put the burden of all these people on me? Did I conceive all these people? Did I give them birth? Why do you tell me to carry them in my arms, as a nurse carries an infant, to the land you promised on oath to their forefathers? Where can I get meat for all these people? They keep wailing to me, 'Give us meat to eat!' I cannot carry all these people by myself; the burden is too heavy for me. If this is how you are going to treat me, put me to death right now—if I have found favor in your eyes—and do not let me face my own ruin. (Numbers 11:11-15)*

This passage is indicative of an entire genre of Hebrew scripture called *lament*. In a lament, a voice of distress is lifted to God. Moses, Job, Elijah, the Psalmists, Habakkuk and many more, all voiced laments to God. The Old Testament contains an entire book of laments (complaints to God) called Lamentations. Imagine that, an entire book in the Bible set aside for complaining!

With that said, we can conclude that complaining had a place in the faith history of the Hebrew people. Therefore, it can have a place in ours, too. It's likely that when we are trying to find our way through the wilderness, a lament is going to find its way from our hearts to our lips.

When it comes of our faith, we are a lot like that "Rant and Rave" section of the paper. We are complainers, but not many of us would really be comfortable owning our complaints to God in front of other believers. We'd rather not sign our names to the complaints.

In the New Testament, John's Gospel tells us that Mary and Martha sent for Jesus because their brother Lazarus was ill. Jesus didn't go to their aid immediately. When He arrived, Lazarus was dead. Mary greeted Jesus with a lament, "Lord...if you had been here, my brother would not have died" (John 11:21).

Mary and Martha expected Jesus, who was a close friend, to be present for them in such a difficult time. It didn't matter to them that Jesus had a reason for tarrying so long. What mattered to them was that Jesus didn't answer their call for help when they asked for it.

We are a lot like Mary and Martha and the ancient Hebrews. We don't like to wait for God to answer our prayers. In fact, we don't like to wait longer than a few minutes to get our food at a fast food restaurant. We like to be waited on quickly. We complain if we get caught at a red light or if the waitress does not fill up our tea glass fast enough. When we don't get what we want, when we want it, we complain. When we think God is at fault, our complaints go straight to God.

Mary complained to Jesus about showing up after Lazarus had died, but please notice her next words to Jesus: "But I know that even now God will give you whatever you ask" (John 11:22). Mary complained, but in her complaint she did not lose her faith in Jesus. She complained, but she remained reverent and hopeful that Jesus could help her in her grief.

When we use complaints as an honest effort to seek God's will and to voice the burdens of our hearts, God hears our complaints and ministers to our needs. This is what we learn from scripture. God has a rant and rave line where we can voice both praises and complaints. Voicing a lament doesn't mean we always get what we ask for, but it does mean that God will listen and that God cares.

There is a big difference in a complaint that seeks change for the sake of justice, fairness, and relief of suffering, and in complaints that are chronic in nature and come from people whose complaints are selfishly motivated.

Chronic complainers always find something wrong with others, whatever the circumstances might be. They are never satisfied with how things are going. In fact, these people make it their job to find the speck in the eye of others while they have a log protruding from their own eye.

Chronic complainers are unhappy people, and they make it their goal to spread their unhappiness to others. They seek to tear down and not to build up. These people are vindictive and hostile and use complaints as weapons to wound others. God is not pleased with the spirit of these people. He wants their spirit to change.

I read a story of a farmer who came to town and told the owner of a restaurant that he'd be able to get him several hundred frog legs to serve if he wanted them. The restaurant owner wanted to know where he'd get so many frogs. "I've got a pond at home just full of them," the farmer replied. "They drive me crazy night and day." The men made an agreement for the farmer to bring him several hundred frogs, and the farmer went back home. He came back a week later with two scrawny frogs and a foolish look on his face. "I guess I was wrong," he stammered. "There were just two frogs in the pond, but they sure were making a lot of noise!"[29]

That's the way it is with chronic complainers. They make a lot of noise. Next time you hear a lot of noise about how bad things are, it may be nothing more than a couple of chronic complainers who have little to do but croak and make noise!

I often wondered how many of the people who phoned or emailed to the "Rant and Rave" section of the paper were chronic complainers, clanging cymbals, people who loved to see their complaints in print, unsatisfied unless they were making a lot of noise.

Whether it be in the church, in the work place, at school, or in a club, it doesn't matter; a complaint can be a catalyst to move forward and make things better. It can keep us from veering off path and getting lost in a wilderness. However, if complaints become chronic, the entire situation can turn toxic. As opposed to lamenting that can lead us to a cleansing of the heart, complaining can lead us to a poisoning of the spirit and the spirits of those around us.

Remember, laments have a place in our faith journey. If you are in the wilderness right now, God will hear your laments and not judge you. You can complain to others in healthy ways as well. However, complaints that attack the character of God and the character of others have no place in our faith journeys. They are harmful and sinful. They do not facilitate positive change.

Prayer

God of All Provisions,

We confess we are constant complainers. We have no patience. We want change to come immediately, and when it doesn't, we lose hope, we lose faith, and we question Your perfect plan.

Teach us the art of lament. Let us come to You in our anger, hurt, confusion, frustration, worry, and disappointment, for we know You are strong enough to handle our feelings. Grant us Your peace so we can wait hopefully, satisfied by Your Holy presence. Let the joy and promise born from the Resurrection be enough for us now.

Only You, God, can fill this void in our hearts. Only You, God, can give us what we wait for. Teach us patience in our longing. Teach us perseverance in our waiting. Let us sit in awe of and not in agitation with Your glorious mysteries yet to be revealed.

Lord, let hope flow through us, hope that one day Your Kingdom will come and we will wait no longer. Energize and inspire us in this waiting so we can participate with You in the building of Your Kingdom here on earth, opposing evil, seeking Your wisdom and serving others in Your Son's name.

Amen.

The Makeover that Matters Most to God

Lent 22

Reality shows come and go these days. One that came but didn't make much of a splash was *The Swan*. Women who qualified for the show had to leave their families for four months to go through a dramatic makeover to improve their looks and their self-esteem, achieved with the help of plastic surgeons, exercise coaches, trainers, dietitians, therapists, make-up artists and others.

The name of the show came from the well-known Grimm's Fairy Tale *The Ugly Duckling*. In this classic children's story, a swan's egg gets mixed in with a group of duck eggs. Larger than the other eggs, it looks out of place from the beginning. After the egg hatches, it's obvious that the "duckling" is different from the others. Life was difficult for the baby swan as the other ducks quacked, "She's ugly. She doesn't look a bit like us. We don't want to play with her." As the story goes, the ugly duckling went through a dramatic transformation as it grew, becoming a beautiful swan, much to the surprise of the other ducklings.

Shows like *The Swan* are tapping into a growing desire of Americans to change the way we look through surgery, exercise, and diet.

I asked a group of grade-school children from the church if they thought appearance is important. The answers varied, but most of the children agreed that it is. To confirm this, I asked the children to raise their hands if they looked in the mirror before they came to church. The only ones who did not raise their hands were a few of the younger children.

I then asked, "Who is your appearance important to?" Surprisingly, they listed their parents ahead of their peers. Of course, they also mentioned themselves.

Why is our appearance important? Our appearance makes a statement. With our appearance we send out messages to people before they get a chance to meet us or know us. With our appearance, we make some kind of first impression.

The conversation with the children took an interesting turn when I asked if their appearance was important to God. Most of the children said they believed God thought appearance was important. Others said that God loves us regardless of what we looked like. This gave me an opportunity to make a few points.

One of these was that we need to love ourselves. Jesus said that we should love our neighbor as we love ourselves. If we don't love who we are, we cannot love others as Jesus commands. Changing something about our appearance sometimes changes how we feel about ourselves. We may have more confidence and have a better self-image after our teeth are straightened or after we've changed how we wear our hair.

However, Jesus once chided the Pharisees for keeping the outsides of their drinking utensils clean while ignoring the dirty insides, a parabolic reference to tending to the body while ignoring our spirits.

When Samuel chose the first King for Israel, he was influenced by Saul's appearance. Saul had an impressive physical appearance. 1 Samuel 9:2 says that he was "without equal among the Israelites— a head taller than any of the others." Unfortunately, Saul's physical stature did little to make him a good king. He was eventually rejected by God as Israel's king, and Samuel began the process of selecting a new king. As he began his search, the Lord said to Samuel, "Do not consider his appearance or his height, for I have rejected him. The LORD does not look at the things man looks at. Man looks at the outward appearance, but the LORD looks at the heart" (1 Samuel 16:7).

So does this mean that our appearance doesn't matter to God? Well, not entirely. God could not care less whether we part our hair in the middle or on the side; whether we have blond, brown, or black hair; whether we have a lot of hair or no hair at all. To the extent that our appearance reflects who we are as a person (our spirit), God *is* concerned.

Often, our appearance communicates how we value ourselves or what we value other than ourselves. We have been made in God's image. Therefore, we should place a high value on ourselves. This includes what we do with our body. Part of what we do with our body is to use it to honor God.

The people of the church of Corinth were profaning their bodies through sexual immorality. The Apostle Paul wrote to them saying, "Do you not know that your body is a temple of the Holy Spirit, who is in you, whom you have received from God? You are not your own; you were bought at a price. Therefore honor God with your body" (1 Corinthians 6:19-20).

For Christians, the body is God's temple. Therefore, our appearance is important. We need to keep the temple in good shape with proper exercise and diet. There's nothing wrong with cosmetic issues either unless we have become slaves to the cultural undercurrents that tell us we are not people of worth unless we look gorgeous enough to enter a beauty pageant.

Outside beauty is wonderful thing. I can appreciate it along with others, but beauty on the inside is what matters most to God. The great makeovers of the Bible had to do with people changing who they were on the inside. Zacchaeus the Tax Collector became Zacchaeus the friend of the people as he returned money to those he had charged too much. Peter, the disciple who denied Jesus the night Jesus was interrogated and beaten, became Peter the great preacher, the Rock. Mary Magdalene, a very troubled woman, became an important friend and follower of Jesus who financially supported His ministry. Saul, the Christian persecutor, became Paul, the missionary to the Gentiles.

These are the kind of makeovers that matter most to God. These are makeovers that have lasting significance. These makeovers change more than appearance.

It's easy to forget that our spirits and our bodies are tightly woven. One has an effect on the other. While it is true that "flesh and blood cannot inherit the kingdom of God" (1 Corinthians 15:50), what we do with our flesh and blood is still of concern to God because the body is His temple.

The temple must be kept holy. It must be kept strong. It must not be profaned by what the eyes see, the ears hear, the hands touch, the mouth tastes, the stomach consumes, or by what passes into the bloodstream.

Jesus was tempted to turn stones into bread in the wilderness. He was famished after going without food for forty days. The bread would have done His body some good. However, Jesus knew that His body and His Spirit were inseparable. What is good for one isn't always good for the other. To have turned the stones into bread and eaten them would have led Jesus into a spiritual wilderness.

Paul rightly said that "our struggle is not against flesh and blood, but against the rulers, against the authorities, against the powers of this dark world and against the spiritual forces of evil in the heavenly realms" (Ephesians 6:12). While the battle is against the underworld, the place of attack is often against the body. We are attacked at our point of weakness: our passions, our drives, our emotions, and our lack of discipline.

These are all used against us as in Hapkido where the martial artist uses circular motions and non-resisting movements to control an opponent. The practitioner avoids having to use strength to overpower an opponent but does so by positioning his or her body in a way that he or she gains leverage and uses the opponent's inertia against him or her. In like fashion, evil simply takes us where we naturally want to go.

In the wilderness, Satan made a play on the weakness of Jesus' famished body in order to get to His Spirit in hopes of putting Him in a spiritual wilderness. He was not successful. He has much more success on us.

Has he had success on you? Take inventory. How are you treating your body, the temple of God? What changes do you need to make to keep the temple of God holy, thus protecting your spirit and keeping yourself out of the wilderness?

Prayer

Lord, we are surrounded by false images of beauty. We let the outward appearances of actors, supermodels, athletes, and beauty queens become the scale by which we measure our worth. We worship this outward beauty and have become slaves to it. God, we are merely fooling ourselves, allowing our fear of rejection to drive our actions. We have abused and manipulated our bodies in order to feel better about ourselves. But the truth is, Lord, there is no amount of plastic surgery, diet plans, shopping sprees, weight lifting, or hair extensions that will get us any closer to You when we are lost in the wilderness. Our bodies are our temples, not because they appear attractive to others, but because they were made to worship You. Let every action we do with the gift of our earthly bodies be for the glory and honor of You alone.

In Christ Jesus we pray, Amen.

Don't Let That Bitter Root Grow

Lent 23

Have you ever noticed that some people don't ever seem to be happy? It doesn't matter if the sun is shining or if it's a stormy day. It doesn't matter if the stock market is up or down. It doesn't matter if their health is good or bad. They are never happy. Not only are they never happy, but also they seem to resent the fact that somebody else in the world might be happy. They make it their mission to make sure others are not.

Somewhere along the way, these people became bitter with life and it oozes out in their speech, in their actions, and even in the expressions they carry on their faces.

Two writers who were bitter rivals were both attending the same party. One had recently had a book published, and the other commented to him, "I read your new book and liked it. Who wrote it for you?" The other replied, "I'm glad you liked the book. Who read it to you?"[30]

Abe Lemons was asked if he was bitter at Texas Athletic Director DeLoss Dodds who fired him as the Longhorns' basketball coach. He replied, "Not at all, but I plan to buy a glass-bottomed car so I can watch the look on his face when I run over him."[31] Do you think he might have been a little bit bitter?

In most cases, bitterness can be traced to some type of loss. People have become bitter after the loss of a loved one, the loss of a job, a divorce, the loss of health, losing a friend, a miscarriage, the loss of a reputation, financial problems or poverty, or an accident. If you are bitter, chances are you have been emptied of something you used to have or you do not have something you always wanted to have and it has soured your spirit.

In the Bible there is a story of a woman named Naomi. She was married to a man named Elimelech, and they had two sons. They moved from Bethlehem to Moab because of a severe famine. While in Moab, Elimelech died. Then Naomi's two sons died. She returned to Bethlehem a childless widow. The women of the city welcomed her home.

"Can this be Naomi?" they asked, a name that means pleasant (Ruth 1:19). But Naomi had become bitter because of her misfortune. She responded. "Don't call me Naomi....Call me Mara, because the Almighty has made my life very bitter. I went away full, but the LORD has brought me back empty. Why call me Naomi? The LORD has afflicted me; the Almighty has brought misfortune upon me" (Ruth 1:20-21).

Compare Naomi's reaction to that of Job following the news of the deaths of his children and the loss of all his property and valuable possessions: "The LORD gave and the LORD has taken away; may the name of the LORD be praised" (1:21). Job reminds us that, in the face of tragedy, a bitter spirit is not a given; it is a choice.

Naomi chose to be bitter. Life had dealt her a very difficult hand. A husband and two sons were dead. But her bitterness only added to her load. You've heard of the expression, "He's got a chip on his shoulder?" It's an adequate expression because a chip is an unnecessary burden that doesn't have to be carried.

Walking through a wilderness can easily cause people to become bitter. We can blame those who caused us to be in the wilderness. We can become bitter that we cannot get out of the wilderness. However, the bitterness only makes the wilderness experience worse. Just think of Moses, who had to deal with the bitterness of the Hebrew people in their wilderness journey.

Bitterness can be directed at God or at others. In Naomi's case, her bitterness was directed at both. Usually we will direct our most bitter feelings toward those we feel are responsible for our loss, but bitterness spills out all over the place and onto others as well.

One employee is bitter against another employee who may be responsible for her not getting a raise or a promotion. A man is bitter toward his ex-wife because he believes she received more than her fair share in the divorce settlement. The second string quarterback is bitter toward the starter because the player took his position. A teenage girl is bitter because she does not have the physical looks her friends have. A retiring man is bitter because he never achieved the status in the community he longed for. A church member is bitter because she hasn't received the recognition she felt she deserved for service she gave to the church.

Bitterness can take root in any of our lives because loss comes to all of us. Not one of us is exempt from experiencing loss. Therefore, all of us are subject to feeling bitter about our losses. Should we discover that we are bitter, we would do well to learn from Naomi because she didn't stay bitter. She had a daughter-in-law, Ruth, who returned from Moab with her, a huge sacrifice of love and commitment. Naomi began to focus on Ruth's needs instead of being consumed with her own bitterness.

Bitter people are focused inward. As bitter people focus on the needs of others, they become less self-centered and less bitter. As Naomi began to focus on the needs of Ruth, she became less bitter. She introduced Ruth to a man who became her husband, Boaz. Ruth and Boaz were married, and they had a son, Obed, the grandfather of King David.

The end of the book of Ruth says that the women said to Naomi, "'Praise be to the Lord, who this day has not left you without a kinsman-redeemer. May he become famous throughout Israel! He will renew your life and sustain you in your old age. For your daughter-in-law, who loves you and who is better to you than seven sons, has given him birth.' Then Naomi took the child, laid him in her lap and cared for him" (Ruth 4:14-16).

Naomi still had grief in her life from the loss of a husband and her sons, but her bitterness was gone. God had brought new life into hers, new purpose, new meaning. God had brought new hope into her life through Ruth, Boaz, and this newborn child.

Helen Keller once said, "When one door of happiness closes, another opens; but often we look so long at the closed door that we do not see the one which has opened for us."[32]

The doors closed in Moab for Naomi, but new ones opened in Bethlehem. She may have never walked through those doors had she not knocked the chip off her shoulder.

If you are holding onto bitterness today, you are hurting others, but mostly you are hurting yourself. You may feel entitled to your feelings. Indeed you may have lost a lot and been injured greatly by others, but your bitterness does you more harm than anyone else. Obey Ephesians 4:31-32: "Get rid of all bitterness, rage and anger, brawling and slander, along with every form of malice. Be kind and compassionate to one another, forgiving each other, just as in Christ God forgave you." God will bless your life, and your wilderness will open to new doors of opportunity.

Prayer

Lord,

Perhaps what we really need is to be known,
For someone to know our desires and our fears,
For someone to know our innermost joy and despair,
For someone to know our struggles and our triumphs.

You know us, God, through and through.
There is no escaping Your sight,
Though sometimes we try to hide behind our bitterness.
You know us even when we make it difficult.

Lord, in Your knowing us, You set us free
From shame, from loneliness, from isolation.
In Your knowing us, You transform our hearts
And allow us to be the loving creation You intended.

Know us this day, this moment,
So we can come before You just as we are
And drink from Your living waters
And know that You, Jesus, are all we need.

Then, help us to share this gift of knowing.
Allow us to know others as You know us.
Help us to live transparently.
Teach us to love unconditionally,
And keep leading us back to Your well every day.

In Christ's Name,
Amen.

Call Me By a Different Name

Lent 24

When I was a boy, our family would "exchange names" for Christmas. Each family member would draw one name out of a hat and the person's name you drew would be the person you would purchase a gift for, which would remain a secret until Christmas Day.

I heard about a very young girl who wasn't familiar with this "exchanging name" tradition. She went with a relative to a family celebration and it was announced that they were going to exchange names for Christmas. The little girl was terribly confused and she protested, "But I don't want to. I like being Emily!"[33]

It's too bad there are not more people like Emily, who like being who they are. I don't mean we should fall in love with ourselves to the point of being narcissistic. The Apostle Paul warned us not to think too highly of ourselves (Romans 12:3). However, we should each have a good healthy self-image. The scriptures teach us to love our neighbor as ourselves. Thus, without proper self-love, we cannot love others properly. A healthy balance needs to be struck.

Finding this balance can be as tricky as riding a unicycle. I'm a unicycle rider. In order to ride a unicycle, you have be in constant motion. Even staying in one place requires movement.

Caring for oneself and caring for others requires a balancing act. Leaning too much toward self-care causes us to fall out of favor with God and others. Leaning too much toward caring for others causes us to burn out, which is not good for self-care. We cease to like who we are and what we've become.

Daniel Bagby, Theodore F. Adams Professor Emeritus of

Pastoral Care at Baptist Theological Seminary in Richmond, Virginia, tells the story of how his mom cared for his father for years after he was diagnosed with Alzheimer's disease. Using his skills as a caregiver, Daniel phoned his mother often and sought to coach her to take the necessary time to care for herself.[34] Caregivers often neglect themselves as they provide care for others.

On one occasion he asked his mother what he might do for her to help relieve some of her stress. Her reply was unique. "When you call me on the phone, I want you to call me by a different name each time" (Bagby).

This strange request made sense only after her explanation. She explained to her son that she could not leave her husband's side without him calling her by name over and over. In a day's period she might hear her name called a hundred times. "Thelma, where are you? Thelma, will you come here? Thelma, don't leave me. Thelma? Thelma, are you in there?" (Bagby) So several times a week Daniel called his mother on the phone and each time he called her by a different name. "Bertha? Is this Bertha Bagby?" Each time his mother would recognize his voice and laugh as they played the game of Thelma being called each time by a different name. These light-hearted moments brought her the relief she needed from the stress of caring for a dying husband (Bagby).

Sometimes we like being "Emily," and at other times we get tired of being "Thelma." Sometimes we like our name and sometimes we wish we could be called by a different name. Sometimes we like the things we do and sometimes we do the very thing we despise doing.

It's difficult to strike the right balance between what we give ourselves and what we give others. Sometimes we are tempted to give up and decide to accept a name that reflects our failures instead of a name that reflects our hopes of what we might become.

Simon was far from being a rock when he first met Jesus. Yet Jesus called him Cephas, or Peter, the first time He met him, a name that means "the rock." Jesus called him by a different name because He saw potential in him that he eventually lived up to.

When Peter denied Jesus three times prior to His crucifixion, those failures could have dictated how he viewed himself from that point on. But when he reconnected with Jesus by the Sea of Galilee after Jesus' resurrection, his balance was restored and his hope renewed. When we connect with God, we can discover a new name that serves as a sign of hope, a release from our pain, and helps us strike the proper balance between caring for self and caring for others.

In the apocalypse of John, the promise is made that on those who endure will be written "the name of my God and the name of the city of my God, the new Jerusalem, which is coming down out of heaven from my God; and I will also write on him my new name" (Revelation 3:12).

So Christians should all live with the hope that one day the call will come from our God and we will be called by a new name. When we hear our new name, we will answer because we will recognize the voice of the one who is calling. He will rejoice and laugh in hearing His voice, for the announcement of our new name will signal that through Christ we have risen above the trials and tribulations of this world, have found our way through the wilderness, and have entered into the New Jerusalem, the city of God.

Prayer

God of Many Names,

We have dual identities in this world...we are both a parent and a child, both a leader and a follower, both a caregiver and a care-receiver. Help us to find a balance in loving and being loved. Let our names on this earth be remembered for our loving actions to others. And let us remember the names of those who have loved us well. Jesus, we confess that it is hard to both love and be loved, and sometimes we do too much of one and not enough of the other. We pray that You will lead us through this wilderness by calling us by the names that are rooted in Your being. Only then can we find our true selves.

In Your perfect name we pray,
Amen.

How Do You
Draw Your E?
Lent 25

A 2006 study by the Kellogg School of Management at Northwestern University found that "possessing power itself serves as an impediment to understanding the perspectives of others." This brings new credence to the saying that you really can't understand a person until you've walked a mile in that person's shoes.[35]

In the Northwestern University study, researchers used a unique method to study the link between power and perspective. They randomly assigned students to two groups. One group was told that they were the group with all the power. The other group was told they had little or no power (Galinsky & Magee). Participants were told to draw the letter "E" on their foreheads. Here is what they found:

> If the subject wrote the E in a self-oriented direction, backward to others, this indicated a lack of perspective-taking. On the other hand, when the E was written legible to others, this indicated that the person had thought about how others might perceive the letter. The results showed that those who had previously been randomly assigned to a high power group were almost three times more likely to draw a self-oriented E than those who were assigned to the low power condition. (Galinsky & Magee)

This research concluded that when you are a person with power you focus too heavily on your own vantage point and it becomes very difficult to even understand the viewpoints of people with no power.

I know a man who was once hired by a company that does billions, yes, billions of dollars of business each year in the garbage disposal industry. What impressed me about this company's philosophy is their training approach. Although this man eventually moved up to an important management position, the company started him out working on a trash truck. For two months, he worked an eight-hour shift, picking up trash. Before moving into the management position, he spent time in every position below him. Company management wanted this man to understand the business from the ground up and the perspective of every employee below him.

Paul says that Jesus came to us in the form of God, but He "made himself nothing by taking the very nature of a servant, being made in human likeness. And being found in appearance as a man, he humbled himself by becoming obedient to death—even death on a cross! (Philippians 2:7-8).

Contrast Jesus' access to power with our own. When we have power, we often use our power for our benefit. We exploit power. We push the throttle forward full speed and channel that power so it benefits us. We want to get all we can for ourselves while the getting is good. We don't think about the consequences that the misuse of our power may be having on other people, whether it's in business, in our relationships, or in our church or denomination. Jesus did the very opposite with His power than we usually do with ours.

Jesus could have exploited His power for His benefit. He had all of God's power at His disposal. Realizing this, Satan made this the focus of his temptations at the beginning of Jesus' ministry.

Jesus had made His way out into the wilderness.

After fasting forty days and forty nights, he was hungry.
The tempter came to him and said, "If you are the Son of
God, tell these stones to become bread." Jesus answered, "It
is written: 'Man does not live on bread alone, but on every
word that comes from the mouth of God.'" (Matthew 4:2-4)

Satan knew that Jesus was in the wilderness contemplating the nature of His ministry. What would be the scope of His ministry?

What shape would it take? What direction would He go? Satan the tempter tried to use Jesus' own hunger against Him. After going forty days without food, Jesus was famished.

What's turning a few stones into bread if you have the power to do so? What's the big deal? This temptation was very subtle, which is the way most of Satan's temptations come to us. If Satan could get Jesus to use His power once for His own selfish benefit, Jesus would have set a precedent for using His power. This temptation was more than about making a meal for Himself out of stones. This was a temptation about abusing power, a temptation to use His power for selfish ends.

Satan uses the same tactics on us. All of us have power to some degree. Whatever degree of power we have, to that degree Satan will tempt us to use it for our benefit and not for the benefit of the common good.

A son who is the favorite of his parents may be tempted to use that position to gain a favorable status in the will.

An executive with insider knowledge may be tempted to feed that information to another person so money can be made in stock trades.

A teenager with access to gossip from Facebook has power to pass that gossip on, or she has the power to let the gossip die without telling it to another soul.

An employee has the power to pull her full weight while the boss is away, or she can cheat and give less than her best, having the attitude, "As long as I can get away with it, I will."

We usually ask, "How is this going to benefit me?" Jesus wants us to ask two questions, "How is this going to benefit the kingdom? How is this going to benefit others?"

These two questions line up with Jesus' two greatest commands: "Love the Lord your God with all your heart and with all your soul and with all your mind'...and 'love your neighbor as yourself'" (Matthew 22:37, 39).

If Jesus had been looking to use His power for Himself, would He have chosen a cross? It was thought that God and a cross didn't belong together, because God is power and a cross is the ultimate submission to those in power.

A cross equals death and death equals weakness. That's the value people equated with instruments of execution. Those who were in the position to place Jesus on the cross saw themselves as the people with the power, the Pharisees, Pontius Pilate, and his Roman soldiers.

As Jesus stood before Pilate, the Jews insisted that Pilate sentence him to death because they said Jesus claimed to be the Son of God.

> When Pilate heard this, he was even more afraid, and he went back inside the palace. "Where do you come from?" he asked Jesus, but Jesus gave him no answer. "Do you refuse to speak to me?" Pilate said. "Don't you realize I have power either to free you or to crucify you?" Jesus answered, "You would have no power over me if it were not given to you from above. Therefore the one who handed me over to you is guilty of a greater sin" (John 19:8-11).

Even while it looked to some that Jesus had lost all His power, there was never a time during the Passion that Jesus did not have access to power.

We are reminded of Jesus' access to power when the soldiers came to arrest Him in the garden of Gethsemane. Peter drew his sword and cut off a soldier's ear, but Jesus rebuked him and then healed the soldier's ear. "Put your sword back in its place," Jesus said to him, "for all who draw the sword will die by the sword. Do you think I cannot call on my Father, and he will at once put at my disposal more than twelve legions of angels? (Matthew 26:50-53).

Jesus had power. He chose not to use His power for selfish reasons, but rather to do the will of God. He chose to use the power of self-restraint. He chose to use the power of love to turn the other cheek. He chose to use the power of forgiveness when He prayed over his enemies from the cross and said, "Father, forgive them, for they do not know what they are doing" (Luke 23:34).

He demonstrated His power from the cross when He gave up his spirit. It wasn't taken from Him. He gave it up. "When he had received the drink, Jesus said, 'It is finished.' With that, he bowed his head and gave up his spirit" (John 19:30). Every one of you has some kind of power. You have power in your relationships with family, in your business, with friends, behind the wheel of a car, in how you use your money, over the words you choose to speak to others, over the attitude you carry to school, in the office, and in the places where you volunteer each week. The question is, "How are you using your power?"

Jesus taught us that our power is not to be used for selfish ends. Power is a gift that should be used for the greater good, for worshiping God with all our heart, soul, mind and strength and for loving our neighbor as ourselves.

If Jesus asked you to draw the letter E on your forehead today based on how you've been using your power, which way would it read? Would it be a self-oriented E or an others-oriented E? As you walk through the wilderness, Jesus wants you to do the same thing He was asked to do 2000 years ago, evaluate how you are using your power. Do you use your power more for yourself, or would your E be drawn where others could read it, insuring that what you care about is their perspective and about serving them?

Prayer

Our Rock and Redeemer Christ,

You walked upon this earth and gave us a Holy Example to follow. You showed us how to love, how to serve, how to be faithful, how to have mercy, how to forgive, and how to use our earthly power to build Your kingdom. We admit these are not new lessons to us. We have heard Your Great Stories time and time again, yet we rarely take Your wisdom to heart, especially in our daily relationships with the ones to whom we are closest. Forgive us for this sin!

Holy Lord, deliver us from the temptation to use our power to serve ourselves and to dominate, manipulate and harm others. Strengthen our wills and cleanse our hearts with Your grace. Teach us a new way of being; carrying out Your compassion in all areas of our lives. Tame our tongues so we do not speak evil against others. Use our voices for the purpose of glory, and not pain. Give us words that comfort, not corrupt. May everything we say and everything we do bring glory to You, God Everlasting.

Amen.

God Will Wipe Every Tear from Our Eyes

Lent 26

By the year 2050, the number of centenarians (those 100 years of age or older) is projected to number 3.2 million. If I'm still living, I'll be a mere youngster at 88 years. One characteristic that all these people will share is that they will all have experienced great loss, for centenarians outlive most of their friends. Most will know what it means to weep.

Weeping is the result of loss, and loss is an unavoidable fact of living. The longer we live, the more loss we will experience and the more tears we shed. People of faith know that Jesus does not insulate the believer from grief.

In John chapter 11, word came to Jesus that his friend Lazarus was sick. Lazarus and his two sisters, Martha and Mary, lived in Bethany, a village just outside Jerusalem. Jesus knew this family well. A messenger was sent to Jesus by Martha and Mary to come to Bethany because Lazarus was sick. The implication was very clear. "Come, so you can heal our brother, Lazarus."

Verse five tells us that even though Jesus loved this family He didn't respond immediately to their request. While He tarried, Lazarus died.

Have any of you ever sat with Martha and Mary? Have you called for Jesus to come in the late hours of the night as a loved one held on for life? Have you called on Jesus for healing after hearing the news that a family member had cancer? Have you called on Jesus for healing only to have Jesus tarry?

Many of you can testify how the Lord has come and brought the healing balm of Gilead with Him, healing you or someone you love. For others, Jesus tarried long enough that grief came to your home. Few experience a wilderness any greater or deeper than where they have to walk life without a loved one.

We know Jesus is a healer. We know Him as the Great Physician. But Jesus doesn't heal everyone. Presumably, Jesus didn't even heal His own father Joseph. We don't have any record of Joseph's death, but we do not hear any more about him after the Passover trip to Jerusalem when Jesus was twelve. It's safe to assume that he died sometime after this. If so, Jesus didn't spare even His own mother, siblings, or Himself from grief.

Jesus will not always shield us from grief, either. Though we may experience healing at times in our lives, we will not be entirely spared from grief. Grief is a part of living. Grief is a result of loving.

This text also teaches that it's okay to express to the Lord our deepest and honest expressions of grief. Martha and Mary did. They expressed to Jesus their dismay that He had waited so long in coming. Both of them said the same thing to Jesus: "If you had been here, my brother would not have died" (John 11:21).

Whereas this is a statement of faith, it's also a statement of grief. In fact, it sounds like anger, a stage of grief many people experience. Their grief was compounded because they believed their brother's death could have been prevented. Jesus could have done something about Lazarus' condition, but He did not.

Death is easier to accept when those we love have lived a long, productive life. When death comes prematurely, grief is magnified. When death comes needlessly, we grieve all the more. Why wasn't he wearing a seatbelt? Why didn't she go to the doctor sooner? Why wouldn't the Lord come to our aid when we called on Him? These questions are questions we ask while we walk in the wilderness.

Grief is not just about death. Grief is also about loss. Sometimes a loss comes by death, but we can grieve the loss of health, the loss of a job, the loss of a marriage, the loss of a good reputation, the loss of a close relationship, to name a few. If we believe others are partly to blame for our loss, it creates anger within us. Before we can move through our grief, we must process our anger.

People who walk in the wilderness of grief have not lost their faith. Mary and Martha both confronted Jesus with their sadness that Jesus had not come sooner. Even so, neither Martha, nor Mary, lost her faith in Jesus. While they had not lost their faith, they held a very honest faith, which is the most healthy kind to have.

> *"Lord," Martha said to Jesus, "if you had been here, my brother would not have died. But I know that even now God will give you whatever you ask." Jesus said to her, "Your brother will rise again." Martha answered, "I know he will rise again in the resurrection at the last day." Jesus said to her, "I am the resurrection and the life. He who believes in me will live, even though he dies; and whoever lives and believes in me will never die. Do you believe this?" "Yes, Lord," she told him, "I believe that you are the Christ, the Son of God, who was to come into the world." (John 11:21-27)*

This passage sits in the middle of John's Gospel. This statement by Martha is the most complete statement in the entire Gospel of the true nature of Jesus. "I believe that you are the Christ, the Son of God, who was to come into the world." When Jesus did not heal her brother, Martha grieved, but in her grief she did not lose her faith in Jesus.

Why didn't she? Because she believed that though her brother was dead he would live again. She believed in the resurrection of the dead. Jesus said to her, "I am the resurrection and the life. He who believes in me will live, even though he dies; and whoever lives and believes in me will never die. Do you believe this?"

Jesus does not spare us from grief. Jesus does not heal everyone, but even those He heals will eventually die. The reason Christians can go to the grave with hope is that we have the promise of Jesus that just because death has come to our bodies, it doesn't mean that we cease to exist. Because we believe in Jesus, even though we die, we will still live. If we live in Christ, it really means that we will never die.

The non-believing world sees this as pie in the sky. The non-believing world thinks that when we are dead, we are no more. Life is over. What you see here is all there is, and there will be nothing for us beyond the grave. Jesus has said otherwise.

> *"Do not let your hearts be troubled. Trust in God; trust also in me. In my Father's house are many rooms; if it were not so, I would have told you. I am going there to prepare a place for you. And if I go and prepare a place for you, I will come back and take you to be with me that you also may be where I am." (John 14:1-3)*

Think about it. Here in this life we grieve. Jesus doesn't save us from grief now. In fact, John 11 teaches us that grief is part of what it means to be human. Jesus showed his humanity when Mary came to Him weeping. She was followed by the mourners, who were also weeping; Jesus Himself was overcome with emotion and He wept. Grief is a normal part of loss, and we should not be afraid of the emotions that come with the grieving process. It is part of the wilderness experience.

But if you want something to shout about, it is this: The Revelation of John says that a day is coming when God will wipe away every tear from our eyes (Rev. 7:17).

As the song by singer Andrae Crouch says of that place to which Jesus has gone to prepare for the believer: "No more crying there, we are going to see the king;/No more crying there, we are going to see the king;/No more crying there, we are going to see the king./Hallelujah! Hallelujah! We're going to see the king."[36]

Contrast this with what Jesus says will happen at the end of the age. "The angels will come and separate the wicked from the righteous and throw them into the fiery furnace, where there will be weeping and gnashing of teeth" (Matthew 13:49-50).

When Jesus called Lazarus from the tomb, it fulfilled what He said to His disciples before they went to Bethany: "This sickness will not end in death. No, it is for God's glory so that God's Son may be glorified through it" (John 11:4).

The purpose of bringing Lazarus back to life had little, if anything, to do with this family being Jesus' friends. Bringing Lazarus back to life was a visible demonstration of the power of Jesus and tangible proof that for those who believe in Him, neither grief, nor death, nor the wilderness will have the last word.

If you are grieving today, my friend, place your faith in the Lord. Cast your burdens upon Him. Live in the promise that a day is coming when every tear shall be wiped away and we shall dwell in the house of the Lord forever. Grief will not have the last word in your life. Even in this life, a day will come when you will be able to walk out of the wilderness and live again. It will never be the same, but by God's grace, you can still find joy, peace, and happiness.

Prayer

For all of those who face death head on,
Through terminal illnesses, fatal injuries, and violence,
Jesus wept.

For all of the caregivers who lost a loved one,
Through the deaths of family and friends, parents, children, and siblings,
Jesus wept.

For those who have loved ones who are lost,
Through Alzheimer's, dementia, mental illness, and addiction,
Jesus wept.

For those who have a severed family,
Through divorce, domestic violence, and uninvolved parents,
Jesus wept.

For those who have lost a sense of self worth,
Through unemployment, financial stress, and major life changes,
Jesus wept.

For those who feel alone in this world,
Through depression, isolation, imprisonment and friendlessness,
Jesus wept.

For those who have experienced trauma,
Through wars, famines, persecution, and torture,
Jesus wept.

Jesus wept. Jesus still weeps today. May His tears comfort us and cleanse our souls as we await God's promise to wipe away every tear from our eyes.

May the peace and comfort of Christ be with us all. Amen.

I'd Rather Be a Tigger
Lent 27

I've come to this conclusion. The road of life WILL eventually carry us into a wilderness. Even as we come to the edge of it and decide, "I'll turn around," we discover that land behind us has already turned into a wilderness. In other words, there is no turning back.

In the midst of the dry, barren land, what choices are left? There are many, but I'd like to address the one we all have: the attitude with which we face the wilderness. If I have a choice between being an Eeyore or a Tigger, I am going to do my best to be a Tigger.

Remember Eeyore? He's that blue donkey in the *Winnie-the-Pooh* book series, technically an Equus asinus, who suffers from an outlook on life that could turn any day of sunshine into a cloudy day. Eeyore's mood could be mistaken for depression by some. He's not depressed. He's just the ultimate pessimist with a case of poor self-esteem. If I were always misplacing my tail, which was held in place only by a small nail that kept slipping out, I might not feel so good about myself either.

Eeyore is a cheerless soul. He talks like he walks, slowly and unenthusiastically. He's never excited about anything. Of course, who would be excited about being in a wilderness? Well, if you think about it, there are a lot of exciting things in a wilderness. It's just not the most comfortable place to be sometimes.

Have you ever tried working with an Eeyore? It's like trying to swim with an anvil tied around your waist. It's like trying to walk up a hill while someone's constantly spraying you with a fire hose. There's just a huge price to pay in negative energy, which drains all the good you are trying to accomplish.

Eeyore's personality opposite is Tigger. He's a tiger, although he's not quite like any other tiger in the jungle. This orange tiger with black stripes has beady eyes and a long chin. His tail, unlike Eeyore's, not only stays attached, but is also used for bouncing. "Bouncy" may be the best word to sum up Tigger's personality, too.

People like Tigger brighten up your day, though they tend to get on some people's nerves, especially early in the morning, before they've had their coffee, or whatever it is that wakes them up. These Tigger people seem to bounce out of bed with smiles on their faces and a spirit of optimism that you'd really like to pour cold water on (either that, or discover the secret to their joy).

You must tip your hat to Tigger, though. His cheerful personality brings out the best in people more times than not. There's an innocence about Tigger that's appealing. He claims he can fly, jump farther than a kangaroo, swim, and climb trees, although he never offers any proof. He also claims that Tiggers never get lost, which he never does.

Some might say that Tigger doesn't live in the real world. Maybe he doesn't. Some might say that he dreams too much. Maybe he does. Perhaps that's why he's such a likable character. Most of us see something in Tigger that's magnetic. We sense that the real world doesn't have the same effect on him that it does on almost everyone else. Either that or he's learned to react differently from the rest of us. That's what endears him to us.

Whatever problems he has, he doesn't allow them to become embedded in his psyche or control his mood for very long. He maintains his bounce. In fact, without his bounce he wouldn't be a Tigger, because "bouncing is what Tiggers do best."

Dr. Randy Pausch was a Tigger. Randy was a dreamer. As a child, he dreamed of playing professional football, authoring an article in the *World Book Encyclopedia*, being Captain Kirk, winning the big stuffed animals at amusement parks, working for Disney, and being in zero gravity.[37]

In September 2007, Dr. Randy Pausch, a Professor of Computer Science, Human-Computer Interaction, and Design at Carnegie Mellon University in Pittsburgh, Pennsylvania, gave a lecture titled "Really Achieving Your Childhood Dreams." The lecture was a part of a lecture series in which top academics were asked to think deeply about what matters to them. They were asked, "Hypothetically, if this lecture were your last, what parting wisdom would you want to leave with the world?"

In Dr. Pausch's case, this was not hypothetical. At age 46, he had been diagnosed with metastatic pancreatic cancer. Even after aggressive treatment that included surgery and chemotherapy, the cancer metastasized and his life expectancy was reduced to a few months.

Partly because of the urgency of the moment and partly because of the dynamic, optimistic personality that Pausch has been known for, the lecture hall was filled with students and staff in anticipation of what he might say. Following the lecture, his presentation was viewed on the Internet by millions and a book was written based on his lecture.

During the hour-long lecture, Pausch used humor, slides, surprise, and story to land his points. Perhaps the beauty of the entire evening was the lightness of it all. Here was a dying man, a deeply intellectual man whose parting words went to the core of the human heart and not just to the intellect. He showed his humanness. Yes, he was sad about his condition, but not bitter. In fact, just the opposite. He was still a man living a life filled with joy, excitement, and passion.

Pausch's simple but profound wisdom included these statements:

"Never underestimate the importance of having fun. I'm dying and I'm having fun. And I'm going to keep having fun every day because there's no other way to play it" (Pausch).

"Experience is what you get when you didn't get what you wanted" (Pausch).

"No one is pure evil. Find the best in everybody. Wait long enough and people will surprise and impress you" (Pausch).

"Brick walls are there for a reason. They are not there to keep us out. The brick walls are there to give us a chance to show how badly we want something. The brick walls are there to stop people who don't want it badly enough" (Pausch).

"We can't change the cards we're dealt, just how we play the hand" (Pausch).

Dr. Randy Pausch was a Tigger. Even in the face of death, he maintained a bounce in his step. Sure, he wept. Sure, he grieved. He was never in denial. He just never became an Eeyore. For him, life was very short, too short. Even though he traveled through the wilderness, he chose to be a Tigger.

Victor Frankl was a Tigger. Frankl, a Jewish survivor of the Holocaust, wrote: "Everything can be taken from man but one thing, the last of human freedom—to choose one's own attitude in any given set of circumstances, to choose one's own way."[38]

Frankl, though surrounded by some of history's worst suffering and some of the greatest atrocities known to humankind, chose an attitude that refused to allow his environment, a wilderness of the worst kind, to dictate his attitude.

The Apostle Paul was a Tigger. He once wrote to the church at Corinth: "I am greatly encouraged; in all our troubles my joy knows no bounds" (2 Corinthians 7:4). Among the troubles he had experienced were beatings, stonings, multiple shipwrecks, as well as dangers from rivers, bandits, his own countrymen, and false brothers. He had labored without sleep and food, and had been constantly on the move. He had known the discomforts of cold and being deprived of clothing, presumably while he was imprisoned. In addition, he faced the pressure and concern for the churches he had started (2 Cor. 11:23-29). Yet Paul's joy abounded.

And if the Apostle Paul had been present at Dr. Randy Pausch's final lecture, his favorite line might have been, "If I'm not as depressed as you think I should be, I'm sorry to disappoint you."

You may or may not have a choice about whether you are in a wilderness, but you do have a choice of how you respond to it. How you respond not only affects you, but also those around you. Will you choose to be an Eeyore or a Tigger?

Prayer

Lord, are we hoarders of Your grace? Do we store it away and keep it all to ourselves? Do we keep Your Good News hidden inside us collecting dust? What good is it, Lord, that we take the light You have given us, and not let it shine?

Even in our times of trouble, Lord, we can still share goodness with others. In our times of wilderness, restore to us the joy of Your salvation. This week, Lord, give us an opportunity for a conversation with a friend, with a neighbor, with a stranger, where we can share joy. Let us remember to laugh, to embrace, to dance and to share. Help us to trust that You are enough, the Gospel is enough, and the Holy Spirit is enough. We merely need to open our mouths and tell the story You have written upon our hearts.

In Christ's name we pray, Amen.

Picking Off the Cockleburs of Life

Lent 28

Bill Irwin was the first blind man to hike through the Appalachian Trail, one of the longest, continuously marked hiking trails in the world. Along with his guide dog, Orient, Bill hiked the 2,167.9-mile wilderness trail from Springer Mountain, Georgia, to Mt. Katahdin in Maine.

The first sign of civilization along the trail comes after hikers descend Blood Mountain. After about thirty miles of hiking, hikers come to Neels Gap. There they find the Walasi-Yi Center, a place for hikers to purchase food and gear. Bill was an inexperienced hiker. In fact, he had never attempted any long distance hikes in his life. By the time he got to Neels Gap, he discovered that it wasn't his blindness that was giving him the most problems, but his feet and the weight of his pack.

Jeff, the proprietor, spent several hours with Bill going through his pack. He helped Bill eliminate obvious things that were weighing him down, like a radio and a tape player. He had a twenty-nine-blade Swiss Army knife that weighed nearly a pound. He swapped Bill's cotton clothes for polypropylene. Jeff put every item on a scale and asked Bill if it was worth carrying. When they were finished, Jeff had helped Bill eliminate twenty-six pounds from his pack.[39]

How much excess weight are you carrying? I'm not asking if you need to go on a diet. This is a spiritual question. When you are hiking through the wilderness, excess baggage must go.

Three guys are hiking through the desert. One is carrying a jug of water. One is carrying a loaf of bread. One is carrying a car door. A man meets each one and asks each one the same question, "Why are you carrying that?" The first man says, "Well, if I get thirsty I'll have something to drink." The second man says, "Well, if I get hungry I'll have something to eat." The third man says, "Well, if I get hot, I'll roll down the window."

If Bill Irwin had been carrying a car door, Jeff would likely have recommended that he leave that at the Walasi-Yi Center. Yet spiritually, there are many people carrying car doors around. People try to please God with good works—car door. People become more concerned about what's on the outside than what's on the inside—car door. People chase after the material and forget to lay up treasures in heaven—car door. People become more concerned about trying to fix other people's problems and don't spend enough time evaluating their own lives—car door. People make religion the "be all and end all" and become legalistic know-it-alls, rigid, harsh, with little grace to offer—car door. People worry about things they cannot control or change—car door.

Life's hard enough without carrying things that weigh us down. But it's easy to pick up our pack and just move on down the trail without subjecting our pack to an objective evaluator. Truth is, we are often blind to what we have in our packs. Even though we've done the packing, sometimes we cannot see all that we've packed and don't realize there's a better way to prepare for the journey.

When I was a boy, I'd often go roaming in the woods around my house. When I returned, it wasn't unusual to have several cockleburs stuck to my socks and my pants. I hated those things. If you don't know what cockleburs are, then you aren't country. My grandfather used to call them porcupine eggs. A cocklebur is an oblong seed with porcupine-like spines that will attach itself like Velcro to animals for locomotion. It doesn't take a genius to decide that cockleburs are unnecessary baggage.

They don't weigh much, but they do make life uncomfortable. These are likely the culprits behind the saying, "He's got a burr under his saddle." When we walk through life's wildernesses, issues come our way at work, at school, in our relationships with friends and enemies that stick to us. If we don't pick off the unnecessary stuff, our lives become filled with objects that weigh us down, or will stick in us and make life uncomfortable.

What's stuck to you that needs to be picked off? What's in your pack that needs to be set aside? Perhaps you are carrying a desire to control everything that happens in your life and in the lives of those around you, especially family. Are you unwilling to forgive? Does the desire for revenge have you weighed down?

Is your load weighted with the inability to be content? Is it self-centeredness or a lack of self-discipline? Perhaps you have a drive for perfectionism that works well for you to a point, but then it becomes a burden. Do you have a need to always be right?

As we move through the day and week, there's stuff that sticks to us. If we don't learn to lay those burdens down, our load gets heavier and heavier to carry. After a while, we strain under the load, and signs of wear begin to show in our bodies, our relationships, our emotions; and we drift from God.

It takes great humility to come in off the trail, pull off our pack, and say to someone, "Please help me evaluate what I am carrying." Peter knew that, so he wrote: "Humble yourselves, therefore, under God's mighty hand, that he may lift you up in due time. Cast all your anxiety on him because he cares for you" (1 Peter 5:6-7).

Blindness humbled Bill Irwin. More than learning to trust his dog, Bill learned to trust God for each step of his life after he went blind. In fact, it wasn't until after he went blind that he learned how to see. That's the message he told our church in Clarkesville back in 1994. Although blindness carried him into a wilderness, he realized that he'd been in a wilderness all along. His blindness was what stopped him long enough to make him evaluate his life and the meaning of life. Thus, the words of "Amazing Grace" became his theme song: "I once was blind, but now I see." That's the message he shared with people he met on the trail.

Not long ago I hiked a difficult section of the Appalachian Trail with my son John. We walked several miles of the trail at night with our headlamps and stopped about midnight. A couple of times as we walked, I turned my headlamp off and walked several steps in the pitch black darkness. I tried to imagine the world that Bill lived in and the faith he had to place in Orient to walk that trail. I realized how easy it would have been to have gotten turned around and lost in the woods. Without Orient, Bill would have had no eyes and no chance of staying on the path.

Even with a guide dog, what Bill did was amazing.

It took a lot of faith to follow God's guidance and attempt to thru-hike that trail, especially for someone who had never hiked before. Yet that's a lesson for all of us. Many of the paths we take in life are first-time paths. As we take them, we need to learn to trust the leadership and guidance of God, because if we attempt to find our own way, then we fool only ourselves; we think we see, but we really don't.

Prayer

Our burdens are heavy in this wilderness, Lord. We have chosen to carry our worries on our own shoulders, becoming slaves to our anxieties. We fill our baggage with old memories of disappointment and hurt, with fear, with egoism. We have fooled ourselves into believing we need these supplies to carry us through our lives!

Teach us the art of letting go. Instill in us those spiritual disciplines that point us back toward You. Replace our hurt with forgiveness, our fear with faith, our pride with humility. Renew in us a lightness of being so that we may walk joyfully among Your glorious creations and move further along Your path.

Amen.

There's a New Road into Barrow, Alaska

Lent 29

If you want to find a true wilderness that's inhabited by people, travel to Barrow, Alaska where the mercury doesn't rise above freezing 247 days out of the year. Located on the edge of the Arctic Ocean, Barrow, population 5,000, is the northernmost town in the United States.

Barrow has been a wilderness for another reason. Over fifty percent of the students in Barrow drop out of school. When they do, they have nowhere to go, literally, because the town is accessible only by boat or air. For 67 days a year, the sun doesn't even rise. The town has dealt with teenage depression, teenage suicide, and even murder. Drug and alcohol use among Barrow's youth is common.

Several years ago, famous NFL Hall of Famer Larry Csonka, traveled to Barrow as a guest speaker for the high school, and the idea to begin a football team at the school was planted in the minds of the students. This was reflected in a survey of the student body conducted by school superintendent Trent Blankenship to determine what activities would help the students remain interested in school. He was surprised at the largest response: form a football team.

In 2006, the Barrow Whalers donned pads for the first time. Mark Voss was named head coach and put on a coach's whistle for the first time in twenty-three years. He surrounded himself with mostly inexperienced men who wanted to make a difference in the lives of over forty young men who needed direction and hope.

Could football really give the teenagers of Barrow hope and direction? The experiment in such a remote part of the world attracted the attention of ESPN, which sent a reporter to Barrow. It was an interesting segment because football in Barrow is as rare as ice hockey in Jamaica. It's not easy to play football where grass doesn't grow; where the practice field is just a player's jog to the Arctic Ocean. In fact, only a few people in the entire town had ever played football before the Barrow Whalers' inaugural season in 2006.

On a Sunday morning in the fall of that year, Cathy Parker was getting ready for church when one of her teenage sons called her to the family room to watch part of ESPN's two-part segment on the northernmost football team in America. When Cathy came into the family room and began watching this segment with her sons, she couldn't believe the players were literally playing on permafrost, the Arctic landscape comprised mostly of rocky soil. Their desire to play and learn the game under such conditions brought tears to her eyes.

The Parker family loves football. Cathy's husband Carl played for the Lowndes County Vikings in Valdosta, Georgia in the early eighties and went on to play for the Vanderbilt Commodores and the Cincinnati Bengals. He was the high school offensive coordinator for his son's football team, the Bartram Trail High School Bears in Jacksonville, Florida. Carl has used sports to teach teenagers, including his three sons, many important lessons about life. His son Kyle went on to have a very successful college career as a quarterback at Clemson University.

On that Sunday morning, Cathy Parker's sons had no idea that God was about to use football to teach their family, and an entire nation, a lesson about faith, vision, hope, and love. After watching more of the ESPN segment, the family loaded up and left for church.

That morning during worship, Cathy kept seeing those players from Barrow, Alaska, playing ball on the hard, rocky surface that stays frozen for most of the year. During that service, God gave Cathy an Arctic-size vision: give those Barrow Whalers a football field, as in an artificial turf field.

Laughter—that's what Cathy got from her three sons when she announced to them after church what God wanted her to do. One of them said, "That's just impossible." They were more right than they knew. Just how do you move hundreds of thousands of pounds of material into a town that has no roads leading into it? This was just one of many unanswerable questions that awaited Cathy as she began to do research for her project. Where would the money come from for such a Herculean project?

Cathy's a smart woman. She's worked in banking. She understands financial matters and has excellent people skills. At the time, her husband worked as the Assistant Recreation Director for St. Johns County in Jacksonville. She used his connections to make the project take off. Carl had just sent out bids for an artificial turf field for the county. Cathy knew she already had a base of contacts for prices and information.

While the project was in its infancy, Cathy was sharing a devotion one morning with her three sons and one daughter. She opened her Bible to Acts 10 and was reading a story about Cornelius, a Roman soldier known for his charitable acts and his faith in God. God wanted to use Cornelius to teach Paul that God doesn't show favoritism, "but accepts men from every nation who fear him and do what is right" (Acts 10:35). God sent others ahead of Cornelius to meet Peter and prepare the way for their meeting.

Cathy explained to her children: "This is God. This is what He'll do for us. He'll go before us and prepare the way for us on our turf project." Cathy says that's exactly what God did every single time.

"There were always obstacles, but God went before us and prepared the hearts of people even before we arrived," says Cathy. "As far as logistics and architecture were concerned, we had the very best in the business to help us, even after being told by one logistics company that moving the material to Barrow could not be done."

Undeterred and faithful, Cathy believed this project would come together in God's timing and in God's way. Remember, football in Barrow was designed to be a tool to help these teenagers overcome social issues. Cathy believed that God was going to use Project Alaska Turf to teach more than x's and o's, too. God was going to use this project to bring hope, real hope of the living Lord, to the teenagers and other people in Barrow. Cathy was determined to help bring these kids out of their wilderness.

That's the reason the entire team from Barrow and their coaching staff were invited to Jacksonville in May of 2007. Cathy's plan was to have players from Bartram Trail High School befriend players from Barrow while coaches befriended coaches. Bartram Trail High School had a Christian coach. Cathy knew the coaches from Barrow would be influenced by him and other coaches while they were in Jacksonville. Cathy told the Barrow coaches if they could get to Jacksonville, the rest of their expenses would be covered. The team did not have the resources. Yet at the last minute, an Alaska businessman stepped forward with $40,000 and paid their way to Jacksonville. God was going before them and preparing the way, just as He prepared the way for Cornelius in the book of Acts.

While the coaches were in Jacksonville, Fruit Cove Baptist Church invited them and all the players to a Sunday service. At the end of the service, the pastor extended an invitation for people to receive Christ. Brian Houston, an African American offensive line coach for the team, responded to the pastor's invitation. He took the pastor's hand and told him he was coming to give his life to the Lord because he'd never seen the love of the Lord the way he had seen it on his trip to Jacksonville.

That night Coach Houston returned to the church to be baptized. Before the baptism, Coach Houston called his grandmother in Alabama and told her of his decision. She could be heard screaming for joy over the phone. She said she had been praying for him for years. Through her prayers, Brian Houston's grandmother had gone before him, preparing the way for his baptism.

By August, the air in Barrow had turned crispy cold. The players donned their pads and began practice for their second season. During this time Cathy Parker continued to work the phones and the Internet, speaking with company executives, logistic companies, and the artificial turf company in Duluth, Georgia. The total cost of Project Alaska Turf had escalated to more than she ever imagined, $800,000. Yet the field her sons told her was impossible to build and logistic companies told her was impossible to deliver, slowly came together. With every phone call and every contact, God was going ahead of her and preparing the way.

Not only did the Barrow Whalers get their field, but they also got their field in time to play their first football game on August 17. Cathy Parker was there to receive her well-deserved praise from the team and from the city.

By kickoff, Project Alaska Turf had received attention from television crews from around the country. Rarely is a sporting event in Alaska national news, much less one in a town of less than 5,000. Yet there was Cathy Parker on the NBC Nightly News being lifted on the shoulders of the Barrow Whalers as they walked onto their new turf. "When you win tonight," she said, "don't throw me into the Arctic."

Even though temperatures were dipping into the thirties by game night, they didn't feel the cold of the August evening either, not with Cathy Parker sitting high on their shoulders. All these players felt the warmth of her love and the love of hundreds of people from across America who sacrificed money, time, and effort, not just to build them a field, but to communicate to these youth from Barrow that they are important, that their lives are precious, that they matter to America, that they matter to God, so they should make every effort to live up to the potential they were created for.

That night, the Whalers won their first game of the season, and they celebrated by jumping into the Arctic Ocean. One player said they were so happy after winning their first game they didn't even feel cold when they jumped in.

This is how one woman and a host of people across America changed the wilderness in Barrow, Alaska. It begins with compassion. It takes a God-sized vision. The Bible says, "Where there is no vision, the people perish" (Proverbs 29:18, KJV). There must be an obedience to follow through with the vision even when others think you must be crazy. There must be commitment and faith to carry out the vision. There has to be an understanding that the vision comes from God and it's God's project, not our own. God changes the wilderness. He just wants to use us to do it.

As Cathy walked the streets of Barrow and met the people of the town, she was greeted like a celebrity. In talking with people, she discovered something that strengthened her faith. Years ago, missionaries traveled to Barrow but had struggled to reach many people or change the social conditions that plagued the town. Many still rely on ancient religious systems where the advice of witch doctors is trusted more than the Bible.

While these missionaries struggled in making a great impact, they succeeded in building a core of believers who have been praying for years that God would send someone to help them, someone to show their youth there is more to life than drugs, alcohol, and dropping out of school. Some were telling Cathy, "God sent you." It occurred to Cathy that God had gone before her to Barrow years ago through missionaries to prepare the way for Project Alaska Turf.

If football in Barrow is as rare as ice hockey in Jamaica, then the artificial turf football field in Barrow is as rare as a skating rink in the middle of the Sahara Desert. What's also rare is the willingness of people to accept visions from God that seem impossible to accomplish. Cathy isn't the only one who receives them. It's much easier to laugh, like Sarah in the book of Genesis, and Cathy's sons at God's visions, than to respond with faith. We say, "That's impossible," and the vision fades. We forget that Jesus said, "What is impossible with men is possible with God" (Luke 18:27).

Today a new road has been built into Barrow, Alaska. It's not a road built over permafrost. It's not the road down to the new artificial turf field. It's not a road for trucks or snowmobiles. The new road to Barrow is the one made to the hearts of the players, coaches, and towns-people. It's the road that's leading people to discover the hope, faith, and love of Jesus. It's not a road into the wilderness, but a road out of it. For Cathy Parker, that's the real vision God gave her in church that day. The new football field was just the tool God used to transport this message to Barrow, Alaska and the Whalers of Barrow High.

Prayer

Lord, we are ordinary and common. Most of us are not famous. Most of us are not wealthy. We are not recognized with magnificent awards. We don't drive fancy cars or live in mansions. Our faces aren't plastered on magazines or on billboards. There are no colleges or universities named after us. Most likely none of us will be the President; most likely none of us will receive an Academy Award; most likely none of us will be remembered three generations after we are gone.

Lord, we are ordinary and common in this wilderness. But, You, God, are extraordinary. Your magnificence thought up the entire universe and You formed it with the command of Your words. Your strength parted seas, moved mountains, and flooded the earth. Your love sent Your Son here to live with us and teach us Your way. Your mercy released the world from death.

Almighty One, through Your awesome power, give us a vision of Your Kingdom-Come. Open our hearts to those crying out for salvation, healing, and justice. Instill in us the creativity, motivation, and persistence to carry this vision into fruition. Through You, God, we can do anything.

Thank You, Father, for enabling our hands to do Your work in this world.

In Christ's name we pray,

Amen.

What's in a Name?

Lent 30

In 2010 I took a three-day safety class that's required to get a motorcycle license. After completing the class, I went across the street to get my license. I had to wait in line to have my photograph taken and to have a new license made. At that point, I got a number, took a seat and waited my turn. Finally, a computerized voice announced, "Now servicing customer number 55 at window seven. Now servicing customer number 55 at window seven."

I sat down in front of the man at the window, and he began to ask me a series of questions: "May I have your social security number, please? Date of birth? Driver's license number? Are you Mr. John M. Helms?" After being nothing more than a number for the first 20 minutes, I was finally referred to by name, not the name I'm usually called, but my name nonetheless. I felt like saying, "John M. Helms? No, my name's Willie Fred Jones."

But it was late in the day and the state employee had already reprimanded a 16-year-old in front of me for wasting his time, so I didn't think he was in the mood for any of my sarcasm.

Have you ever felt like just a number in this automated world? Have you ever felt like a nameless face in the crowd? Why does it matter so much that others know us by name?

Deep down we know that unless someone knows us by name, there can be no real depth to the relationship.

Suppose a man sees a woman across the room, and he's smitten by her beauty. He notices she is not wearing a ring, which could mean she's not in a relationship. He gets up enough courage to invite himself to her table. What do you suppose will be the first things he will want to learn about her? Social security number? Date of birth? Driver's license number? I don't think so. He wants to know her name.

Suppose he sees her the next day and says, "Hey, girl from the table who talked to me yesterday." Do you think that's going to send her a very positive message? He should at least remember her name.

Until we can affix a name to someone, there is something significant about that person that is missing. A huge part of one's personality is built around a person's name. We cannot build and shape an identity around anyone until we know that person's name. Until others know us by our name, there is a barrier that is likely to exist between them and us.

Thus, when Moses came face to face with God in the wilderness and heard God speak to him from a bush that was ablaze but was not being consumed, he wanted to know this God by name.

Moses heard God telling him to return to Egypt to lead the Hebrews out of slavery and out of Pharaoh's control. If he was to go on this mission in Egypt to rescue the Hebrew slaves, as God wanted, whom was he to say he was coming on behalf of? What God was he representing? Moses wanted to know God's name. Moses wanted a relationship with this God; otherwise this mission was doomed from the beginning.

God gave Moses an interesting answer. He answered with a verb and not a noun.

Names are typically nouns. God's name is a verb. He responded with a Hebrew word, "Yahweh." The translation is difficult to capture in English, but here are some stabs at it: "I am who I am" or "I will be who I will be." I especially like this one: "I will be there."

From the time Moses and the Hebrews left Egypt, God was there. Otherwise, they would never have been freed from Pharaoh's control at all. Once freed from Egypt, the Hebrews saw God's presence in the form of a pillar of cloud by day and a pillar of fire by night to guide them in the wilderness.

God was there when the Red Sea parted and the Hebrew people went through on dry ground and crossed to the other side. When the water at Marah was bitter, God was there and He made the water sweet. When they traveled through the Desert of Sinai and grumbled against

Moses because there was no food, God was there and provided manna and quail to eat. When they camped at Raphidim and there was no water and the people quarreled against Moses, God was there and provided water from a rock. When the Amalekites attacked the Israelites, God was there and used Joshua to lead the people to defeat them. To remind the people that Yahweh was there, Moses built an altar and called it "The Lord is my Banner."

Moses went up on Mount Sinai and the Lord was there. Because of the Lord's presence, the Bible says that the mountain was covered with smoke which billowed up from it like a furnace, and the whole mountain trembled violently. When Moses came down, the people knew he had been with God. Up on the mountain Moses had received the words from God and wrote them on tablets; we know these words as the Ten Commandments.

As Moses and the people traveled through the wilderness, the tabernacle, also called the Tent of the Meeting, traveled with them. The tabernacle represented the very presence of Yahweh.

We are no different than the ancient Hebrews. We also need to be reminded of the presence of God. We live in a world where there is evil all around and sometimes in us. I think we have the idea that if we are basically good people, all should be well and we will be blessed. There should be no problems. There should be no pain. Everyone should have a job. All the bills should be paid. The children should be succeeding. The marriage should be strong. Our health should be fine. If the Lord is here, we think, then the Lord ought to make everything peaceful and right.

God never promised us anything like this. He never promised that life would be easy. Moses discovered that his journey with God included a wilderness. Although Moses was experienced in the wilderness, I think he expected his journey with all those people to be a brief journey through the wilderness, nothing lengthy.

That's where you and I are like Moses. None of us expect lengthy journeys through the wilderness. For some of us, even a brief journey may cause us to question God.

Yet what Moses found, and what Moses can teach us, is that Yahweh was with him in the wilderness. Moses had met God there. Moses knew that if God were to abandon him, there would be no hope for him or those he was leading. So he held onto the promise of Yahweh, "I will be there."

> *Moses said to the LORD, "You have been telling me, 'Lead these people,' but you have not let me know whom you will send with me. You have said, 'I know you by name and you have found favor with me.' If you are pleased with me, teach me your ways so I may know you and continue to find favor with you. Remember that this nation is your people." The LORD replied, "My Presence will go with you, and I will give you rest." Then Moses said to him, "If your Presence does not go with us, do not send us up from here. How will anyone know that you are pleased with me and with your people unless you go with us? What else will distinguish me and your people from all the other people on the face of the earth?" And the LORD said to Moses, "I will do the very thing you have asked, because I am pleased with you and I know you by name." (Exodus 33:12-17)*

Moses had come to understand the very essence of the nature of Yahweh, "I will be there." Moses had come to understand that unless God was there with him, he had no business representing God anywhere. Unless God was with him, he was no different from any other person in any of the places in the Promised Land they were promised to inhabit.

The one thing that distinguished Moses from others is that God knew him by name and that he knew God to be a God of action, a God interested in the people's day-to-day needs, issues, and problems.

That hasn't changed since the days of Moses. God knows each of us by name. He knows when we are like the Hebrews moving through the wilderness, struggling, complaining, quarreling, afraid, in awe, defeated; he knows when we've sinned and when we are worshiping.

Since the name of God has not changed, we can each know God. He has promised to be with those who invite Him to be a part of their lives. He doesn't force His way in. He politely stands at the doors of our hearts and knocks.

When you wake in the morning, does the Presence of God go

with you? God will go with you if you asked Him to, humbly confessing your sins and asking Him to direct your life. However, if we live with the attitude, "I've got this. I can handle this," we might as well be a number and one day instead of hearing our names called, the Bible says that instead, Jesus will say, "I never knew you; Away from me, you evildoers! (Matthew 7:23).

Prayer

God Who Is With Us,

Holy, Holy, Holy is Your name!
Your promise is sure!
Your revelation, perfect!
You call us by name,
You call out to us in this wilderness.

Who are we to receive Your invitation?
Who are we to dwell in Your presence?
We neglect our own people,
Allowing injustice to rule nations.
We worship idols and ideologies,
We serve the gods of celebrity.
We abuse Your creation,
And ignore its cry for redemption.

Let Your presence purify our hearts.
Let the Truth in Your Son save us from sin.

May the God who calls out to His people
Receive His children under His wings.
May the Lord who is with us
Hear His children cry out His name.

Amen.

What's on Your Bucket List?

Lent 31

In the movie *The Bucket List*, Jack Nicholson and Morgan Freeman play the roles of two aging men who both get the news that they have terminal cancer.

Nicholson plays Edward, a wealthy owner of numerous hospitals who is primarily interested in making lots of money. He's terrible at relationships. He's been married four times and is estranged from his only daughter. He is at the center of his world. Those who work for him understand that their job is to please him.

Freeman plays the role of Carter, a mechanic whose lifelong dream was to become a history teacher. All that changed with an unplanned pregnancy. He had to drop out of college, get married, and begin supporting a wife and child. For the next 45 years, he worked at that same repair shop. He sent his children to college, giving them the dream he never had. He's a man of deep faith. He had never been unfaithful to his wife, but as the years passed, the passion in the marriage began to fade.

These two men—one black, one white—are opposites in nearly every way. They have two things in common: they know that they have less than a year to live and they've ended up sharing a hospital room. Each has to decide what he will do with the time he has left.

Before leaving the hospital, Edward discovers on the floor a wadded up piece of paper that Carter had attempted to throw in the trash. On that paper, Carter had written down some things he wished to do before dying:

1. Help a Complete Stranger.
2. Laugh Till I Cry.
3. Drive a Shelby Mustang.
4. Witness Something Majestic.
5. See Rome, the Pyramids, Masada, Hong Kong.

When Edward starts reading his list, Carter protests, but it is too late. Carter explains that making such a list was required in his freshman philosophy class as an exercise in forward thinking. The teacher called it "The Bucket List" because the list was supposed to contain things they wanted to do in life before they "kicked the bucket." Carter said he was just redoing his list.

Edward starts having fun at Carter's expense. He starts adding his own items to the list like "skydiving" and "kissing the most beautiful girl in the world." When Carter asks him how he proposes to do that, Edward says, "Volume." The next thing he adds to the list is "Get a tattoo."

Edward begins to get excited. Then he says, "We can do this. We should do this." Carter tells him he is crazy. "The list is meant to be metaphorical," he says. Edward begins to get to Carter when he asks him if he is simply going to go home and allow people to gather around him and watch him die.

By the time Carter's wife makes her way back to the room to receive the bad news that his cancer is terminal, Carter has decided he's given his entire life to his family, and perhaps he has actually earned a little bit of time for himself. Before he dies, he wants to mark a few of these things off his list. He and Edward are going on a trip.

The rest of the movie follows these two men as they check items off their lists, and as they do, they continue to ponder what is really significant about life.

We all have a list of things we want to do before we die. Some of you have a list of things you want to do; you are just so young you haven't even thought about dying. You are fortunate enough not to have grieved the death of someone close to you, so life hasn't yet jerked you into the reality that we are mortals.

Others of you know death because it has struck close to home. You have grieved the death of friends and family. Perhaps you have actually come face to face with your own mortality.

The Psalmist wrote:

"A thousand years in your sight are like a day that has just gone by, or like a watch in the night. Yet you sweep people away in the sleep of death—they are like the new grass of the morning: In the morning it springs up new, but by evening it is dry and withered" (Psalm 90:4-6).

"The days of our life are seventy years, or perhaps eighty, if we are strong; even then their span is only toil and trouble; they are soon gone, and we fly away (v. 10). "So teach us to count our days that we may gain a wise heart"(v. 12).

When Edward started making his list, Carter told him that he'd taken a bath deeper than his list. How many people do you know who are living lives with lists that are nothing more than lists of pleasure, lists designed to build up the ego, lists which focus on the material, the superficial, and the inconsequential, lists filled with things that are passing away?

We need to count our days. We need to have wise hearts. Because you are reading this book, I know you are contemplating some very serious spiritual decisions in your life. Perhaps your bucket list will be one of them.

We all have a wish list of things we want to do in life, but how many of us are putting off significant things that we need to be doing now?

When the father of a good friend of mine died, he said he had no regrets about the relationship he had established with his father over the last several years. While he grieved over his father's death, he had a peace in his heart because he had not put off the significant things with his father he needed and wanted to do. I've known many others who've had to live with regrets of days they cannot get back with people they love.

If God were to take us up on the mountaintop today like He did Moses before the end of his life and show us the landscape that lies before us, we would all see things we still want to do before we die. Moses wanted to cross over into the Promised Land. He could see it. He had lived about 43,800 days of life, but God said, "You shall not cross over there."

The danger of putting off what needs to be done now is that none of us are given any assurance of time, not even the next minute. We have only so many days and none of us know the number.

Part of the grief associated with the end of our lives is the realization that we are leaving some things undone. Some of that may be because of missed opportunities, wasted time, or wrongly chosen paths.

Nevertheless, not getting everything done we want to get done may not be all bad, if we are living in such a way that at the end of life, we still have some spiritual vigor left that continues to drive us to set new goals and dream new dreams. Let's live in such a way that even if we don't get to scratch off everything on our list, we've lived lives that have inspired others to take up the causes we've championed, and make them their own. That's what Moses did for Joshua. Maybe others will do that for us.

Evaluate your list; make changes where you need to make them. Live in such a way that when your time is up, others will want to carry on the work that you did not complete, for your family's sake, for the community's sake, for the church's sake, and for the kingdom's sake.

Prayer

God through Life and Death,

Help us to remember that it is not how much we do in life, but how we do it; it is not who we know but how we treat them; it is not what we accomplish, but whom and what we serve in our endeavors that matters to You. May our daily work be pleasing in Your sight, and may our life's work be carried out in our daily living.

Amen.

People Don't Forget
What You Are Made Of
Lent 32

I know of only one trade that my grandfather, Benny Frank Baker, made where he came out ahead. He never could have made a living as a horse trader in his younger days. I've seen more than one person take advantage of my grandfather's generosity. So I was surprised one day to hear him pull out a story from the 1940s or '50s, a time in life when he wasn't as concerned about his fellow man as the person he later became.

He recalled the days when farmers would buy up feeder pigs called shoats, feed them out for a couple of months, and then sell them for a profit. One man in the community, more than all the others, had a reputation for turning good profits on shoats. One day my grandfather asked him for his secret. He was told that the day before he sold his pigs he fed them all the sweet potatoes they would eat. After they were stuffed with potatoes, he filled up the troughs with water and syrup. The hogs gorged themselves on the sweet water. With their bellies full of potatoes and syrup water, he took them to the sale.

Some time later my grandfather had some young shoats for sale. He went to town to see if he could find a buyer for them. As fate would have it, the first person he saw was the man who had given the secret. He asked the man if he'd like to buy his shoats. The man told him he'd come out the next day and take a look at them.

That night my grandfather fed those shoats all the sweet potatoes they could eat and then carried water and syrup to the trough until they were fat as plums. The next day the man came out to look at the pigs and bragged about how good they looked. He bought them and carried them away.

Some time later the two men met again. The buyer, who knew he'd been taken at his own game, told my grandfather that he fed those pigs out on peanuts for two months and when he sold them, he still lost money. Laughing, my grandfather told him that he'd followed his prescription for fattening up the pigs just like he taught him.

The story of his younger days is a reminder that the temptation to sell our integrity is high. Integrity is a virtue in which a person strives for truth, shows consistency of character, and works hard to ensure there is no incongruity in one's words and deeds. A person of integrity realizes there is a cost to integrity, but there is a greater cost involved when integrity is sacrificed. Integrity is doing what is right, even when no one is watching.

One very inspiring example of integrity was highlighted in a 1998 Georgia House of Representatives resolution praising the accomplishments of Cleveland Shroud, a well-known coach and educator who was employed by the Rockdale County Board of Education for 39 years before his retirement in that year. The resolution noted many awards bestowed on Coach Stroud: Citizen of the Year in Rockdale County twice, the Georgia Optimist Club's Georgian of the Year, and the Jack Kelly Fair Play Award from the U.S. Olympic Committee. The resolution noted his excellent career in public education, his devotion as a member of Macedonia Baptist Church and the local chapter of the NAACP, and his election as the first black to the Conyers City Council.[40]

The resolution also noted Stroud's integrity and mentioned one notable example that surprised the Georgia High School Sports Academy. In 1987, Stroud coached the Rockdale County High Bulldog basketball team to 21 wins and 5 losses to qualify for the state playoffs (Rivers).

They moved through each bracket of the playoffs and capped the season with a come-from-behind win in the final game to claim the state championship. Only later did Coach Stroud discover that he had an ineligible player on his team. The player wasn't a starter. He wasn't a regular substitute. In fact, this player played only 45 seconds of one game in which the team was ahead by 23 points. Only after the season did the coach learn that the student had passed only four out of six courses the previous fall, one short to be eligible (Rivers).

What would you have done? The 45 seconds the player played didn't affect the outcome of the season. Yet rules were broken. Here's what Coach Stroud did. He wrote the State Athletic Association to inform them of the infraction. Then he wrote the local school board. Next he addressed the student body and explained what had happened and why the school had to forfeit the state championship, even though they earned it.

In "A Morality Tale" by Paul Greenburg, Coach Stroud said, "You've got to do what's honest and right and what the rules say. I told my team that people forget scores of basketball games; they don't ever forget what you are made of."

These prophetic words were affirmed in Georgia House Resolution 1367. I doubt any of the legislators could remember the score of the championship game that Rockdale ultimately forfeited, but they knew that Cleveland Stroud was a person of integrity. They knew what he was made of. Proverbs 22:1 says, "A good name is more desirable than great riches; to be esteemed is better than silver or gold." I'd hate to leave this world with people remembering me as the man who made lots of money off shoats by feeding them potatoes and sweet water. My grandfather didn't leave the world that way either. In fact, I knew him as a man who gave to those who asked and did not turn away from the one who wanted to borrow (Matthew 5:42).

He never had much. I don't think my mother could have purchased a very expensive car with what she inherited from her father. He didn't leave much if you measure his life by those standards. However, take a ride through Barbour County, Alabama, and stop and ask some folks if they knew Benny Frank Baker and watch their faces light up.

Then get ready to hear some stories. You'll know Benny Frank spent his time building a good name. He didn't get off to a fast start, but he finished strong. Like Secretariat, the 1973 Triple Crown winner, he had a great kick.

I don't meet a lot of people who haven't been through a wilderness. Sometimes it's of their own creation. They made decisions they'd like to forget: times they've sacrificed their integrity, given into temptation, and chosen the wrong road. It would be nice if everyone could be recognized for being a Coach Stroud, but we don't always make the right decisions.

The truth is, most of us will live lives like my grandfather, quiet lives, meaningful lives, filled with mistakes, but also, with second opportunities.

The question is, what will we do with the second chances we have? My grandfather left a great legacy. My family remembers the wilderness because it's part of what shaped him. Along with everyone else, we also remember him for how he came down the stretch. He finished strong.

Prayer

Lord,

What will we do with our second chances in life? Will we squander these grace-filled opportunities? Will we pass them by, ignoring their value? God of New Life, we confess we have wasted enough time dwelling on the past. We have wasted enough days repeating the same mistakes. Deliver us from our mediocrity!

Instill in us a new way of being. Give us discomfort in our lives to incite change in us. Turn our lives upside down! Teach us how to live honestly, purely, simply and graciously. Renew us, inspire us, motivate us and guide us.

In Your divine mercy,

Amen

Jesus' Favorite Place

Lent 33

Where is your favorite place? If you could be any place right now, where would you be? Would you be seated in a beach chair watching the sun move below the horizon while the waves gently lap at your feet? Would you wake up to a cup of hot coffee, walk out on the balcony of a log cabin in the North Carolina mountains and look at the early morning fog as it brushes against the mountain peaks? Would you go back in time, perhaps to a place in your childhood where life seemed simpler, freer, and unencumbered by life's stresses and pressures?

I'm convinced that some people's favorite place is Wal-Mart. My dad has said that when he dies he wants to be cremated and have his ashes spread in Wal-Mart because he knows my mom will go visit him at least twice a week.

Where was Jesus' favorite place? Was it His boyhood home in Nazareth where He learned how to use a saw and a hammer alongside His father in the carpenter shop? Perhaps His favorite place was the Synagogue. The Bible says that it was Jesus' custom to go to the Synagogue. He went there as a twelve-year-old child with His parents and that's where they found Him after being separated from them for three days. He went there often as an adult to worship and to teach.

It could have been Caesarea Philippi, a place north of the Sea of Galilee. This was a remote place where He carried His disciples to escape the crowds. There the springs of the Jordan River bubble from the earth and join waters that flow down from the melted snow of Mount Hermon. There Peter made his great confession: "You are the Christ, the Son of the living God" (Matthew 16:16).

Some of you might say that Jesus' favorite place was among the people—not just religious people, but even among people who had no religion. Jesus loved all people, even those who lived lives that did not reflect a faith in God—sinners, in other words. Jesus was often found at parties and gatherings where people were celebrating life. He was criticized for being found in such places.

You can make a good argument that Jesus' favorite place was the Sea of Galilee. He spent the majority of His ministry there. He called His first four disciples from the beach. He wanted to take fishermen and make them fishers of men. Many of His miracles were performed next to the Sea of Galilee. He spoke to the waves and they became still. He multiplied a couple of loaves of bread and a few fish to feed thousands of people by the Sea of Galilee. He healed a crazy man who lived among the tombs in a village by the sea.

I don't know that I would argue with any of these, but I think one could make a good case that Jesus' favorite place was The Mount of Olives. The Mount of Olives is a ridge that runs for a two-and-a-half-mile stretch east of Jerusalem and is high enough to give a view of most of the city.

Olive groves lined this hill in the days of Jesus, and some ancient trees still dot the hillside today. This hillside provided beauty, perspective, rest, relaxation, a place to withdraw from the people, and a place to talk with and teach His disciples. It was a place to think, a place to pray, a place to make decisions. We all need a place like this, don't we? Perhaps you have found such a place to read this book.

Some of the most significant events of Jesus' ministry took place on the Mount of Olives, both joyful and tragic. He often spent the night there after a day of ministry in the city. Jesus paused there during the event commonly called the Triumphal Entry and looked over the city as He wept for the people. On the Mount of Olives, He predicted that Peter would deny Him. There He prayed and agonized over the cross, and "his sweat was like drops of blood falling to the ground" (Luke 22:44). He used the Mount of Olives as a classroom for His disciples. He scolded His disciples for not laboring in prayer with Him as He agonized over the decision that was before Him. It was on the Mount of Olives that Judas betrayed Jesus.

His ministry had begun in the wilderness, literally. He went to the wilderness, and it was there that He determined the kind of ministry He would embrace. He resisted the temptation to use His power to overcome in a spectacular manner. The wilderness He was experiencing on the Mount of Olives seems to have been the agony of any man who knew the kind of physical suffering he was about to endure but could not avoid.

It interests me greatly that Jesus chose to take His disciples back to the Mount of Olives to experience His ascension into heaven and to announce the gift of the Holy Spirit. Why did He choose this place? The disciples would have remembered the good times in that place—restful and peaceful times when they sat around and listened to Jesus teach them. But their memories may have been dominated by the painful moment of Jesus' arrest as Judas betrayed Him with a kiss.

Perhaps this spot was chosen to balance the pain of that night when Peter, James, and John could not stay awake to pray with Jesus. In going to the Mount of Olives for His ascension, Jesus turned the tears and the sweat drops of blood shed there in agony into tears of joy, into a service of empowerment through the gift of His Holy Spirit, and as a commissioning service for them to go and be His witnesses in Jerusalem, in all Judea and Samaria, and to the ends of the earth. In meeting there for the ascension, Jesus redeemed both the place and His disciples.

Wherever Jesus' favorite place was, I think I know where His favorite place is. It is in the hearts of people who want to sit at His feet and learn His ways. His favorite place is among sinners who are looking for mercy and forgiveness. Jesus wants to abide in us and journey with us to our favorite places in this life and also to the painful places where forgiveness can restore our spirits, to places where old teachings can be further understood, to places where new words of encouragement and teaching can be received, to places where we are blessed with the Holy Spirit and commissioned anew to serve the Lord.

Prayer

We have a place on the shore, Lord,
By the Sea of Galilee
Where You call us to follow You,
Setting us captives free.

We have a place among the crowds, Lord,
To experience Your mysterious word,
To ask questions in our curiosity
And ponder all we have heard.

We have a place on the mountain, Lord,
To be with You as we pray,
To be with You in our agony,
To speak what we cannot say.

We have a place at Your table, Lord,
Where we each sit at Your side
To share a meal, a drink, a memory,
And discard our divisive pride.

We have a place in Your Kingdom, Lord,
To complete Your work on earth,
To love, to give, to serve, to share,
To make the least the first.

We have a place in Your heart, Lord,
As You have shown us by Your grace.
Now let us open our hearts to You,
So You may fill that barren space.

Amen.

Downward Mobility

Lent 34

In the last few years the economy has made the phrase "downward mobility" too familiar for too many people. To a person trying to make a living, it means taking a pay cut, losing benefits, or perhaps losing a job altogether. That might result in selling the boat, living with a less expensive car, or in some cases having to accept help from others to make ends meet.

To an athlete, downward mobility means the body no longer functions at the same level of performance. The stamina is not as great, the muscles will not lift as much weight, and the legs will not run as far or as fast. To the aging person, downward mobility may mean that one is more forgetful, less mobile, and more dependent on others. It may mean handing over the car keys, leaving one's home for a care facility, or giving up one's decision-making power to someone else.

Downward mobility is not a very welcome part of life. I'd like to see if I can change your mind by telling you a story about Henri Nouwen. Nouwen was born and educated in Holland. As an adult, he was ordained as a priest in the Roman Catholic Church. *The Wounded Healer* may be his most well-known book. Nouwen believed that it's out of our brokenness that we are able to empathize with others, listen to them with love and compassion, and help bring healing to them.[41] But it is his little book titled, *In the Name of Jesus*, the last book he wrote before his death, that contains his reflections on downward mobility.

Please understand that Father Nouwen became quite famous as a professor, writer, and priest, and achieved celebrity status among his peers. He climbed the ladder of success. He could have written his own ticket to almost any teaching position in his profession. Yet as he entered his fifties he came face to face with whether becoming older brought him closer to Jesus.

"After twenty-five years of priesthood I found myself praying poorly, living somewhat isolated from other people, and very much pre-occupied with burning issues. Everyone was saying that I was doing well, but something inside was telling me that my success was putting my own soul in danger."[42] Nouwen was in a wilderness.

That's not a message that is preached every day. Success is to be celebrated, isn't it? Success is what we work for, isn't it? Don't we play ball to win championships? Aren't we in business to make money? Don't we teach to produce scholars? Doesn't Jesus want us to succeed? Don't we pray for our children to succeed? Well, of course. All of us want to succeed. Here's a deeper question: "Can success lead us into a wilderness?"

Left unchecked, success can change us for the bad as much as it can change us for the good. There are temptations that come with suc-cess, and every day there are people who crash and burn because they do not handle it well. For Nouwen, the temptations of success had begun to pull him in ways that were unhealthy.

Jesus dealt with temptations like that. It's interesting that the tempter came to Jesus at the very beginning of His ministry to tempt Him with success. Note that Jesus made up His mind *before* His ministry became successful how He was going to deal with His success.

Jesus was in the wilderness on a spiritual retreat of sorts, fast-ing and praying.

> *Then the devil took him to the holy city and had him stand*
> *on the   highest point of the temple. "If you are the Son of*
> *God," he said, "throw yourself down. For it is written: 'He*
> *will command his angels concerning you, and they will lift*
> *you up in their hands, so that you will not strike your foot*
> *against a stone.'" Jesus answered him, "It is also written,*
> *'Do not put the Lord your God to the test.'" (Matt. 4:5-7)*

What test? What temptation was it that Jesus was confront-ed with? The temptation of power and the temptation of success.

As defined by whom? As defined by all those who would have witnessed such a spectacle.

Satan thought Jesus might be a needy person, needing to hear the accolades of the crowds, needing to hear them call out His name. This would have only set the stage for Satan to tempt Jesus with yet another self-indulging feat. Jesus would not have any of Satan's ploys. Jesus would not allow Satan to define success for Him.

Nouwen came to realize that all his colleagues were defining success for him. As a writer, his books were selling. So he was successful. As a speaker, he was in demand. So he was successful. As a priest, He would have been welcomed in any parish. So he was successful. As a professor, he could have had his choice of Catholic schools. He had success in the classroom. All of this was good. "So where's the temptation?" you ask. I suppose it was to continue to be the Nouwen that others wanted him to be.

When we allow others to define our direction instead of Jesus, even if our direction is successful by the world's standards, we've taken the road most traveled, which is not the road Jesus typically calls us to take.

Evil can be subtle. Satan is at his best when hiding the hook. Jesus always saw the hook and Satan never got to Him. He could not even use Jesus' success to trick Him.

But Satan has been very successful in using the success of others to cause many to stumble. I am not immune and neither are you.

We are fools if we only think that Satan always wants us to fail. One of Satan's great game plans is to root for us to succeed because success, even more than failure, can be the temptation that lures us away from making the Lord Jesus, the one who gives us abundant life, the most important part of our lives.

If our success lures us away from Jesus, then Satan's all for our success. Success can become our god.

So God wants us to fail? Of course not. God wants us to succeed, but God says that there can be no other gods before Him. We must strive to succeed, but not worship success. We must be sure that the drive for success does not find its way between us and God.

Although Henry Nouwen was successful by the world's

standards, he had uneasiness in his soul. That's interesting because he was doing good things.

Once we accept Christ and choose to follow Christ, we must constantly choose and reevaluate how we will serve Him. What choices will we make day after day that will culminate in choosing the better of two paths? Which voices will we listen to? How will we define success?

Henry Nouwen left Harvard, where some of the world's best and brightest minds teach and study. He left there and moved to L'Arche, a community for mentally handicapped people, and began working as a house parent to those impaired adults.

Ironically, to keep his spiritual life from tail-spinning, he chose a life of downward mobility to the "least of these." There, no one knew him. No one had read his books. His name meant nothing to the residents. He did not impress anyone, and since I.Q. was not high among many of the residents, his twenty years at Notre Dame, Yale, and Harvard did not make it worth mentioning in a day's conversation.

In a move of downward mobility, Henry Nouwen learned to see himself in a new way. Having all of his successes stripped from him by a group of mentally handicapped people who cared little for books, degrees, and honors, Nouwen realized that the common denominator in life is the ability to give and to receive love, regardless of any accomplishments. For him, the experience was freeing.

And it should be for us, too. Regardless of whether we have achieved great successes by the world's standards, each of us has the ability to give and receive love.

Failure can sometimes dam up the channels of giving and receiving love. We can be ashamed or embarrassed, or others can reject us and withhold forgiveness. But success can be equally as damaging. We can become prideful and arrogant. We can push God and others away and simply decide that we can live our lives on our own terms.

Look at how Jesus handled success. Toward the end of His ministry He rode into Jerusalem to the cheers of a great crowd. They broke off palm branches, laid them in the streets, and shouted, "Hosanna to the Son of David! Blessed is he who comes in the name of the Lord" (Matthew 21:9).

If you had asked His disciples that day what they were feeling, they would have said, "Ah, success! This is what we've been waiting for. The Kingdom isn't far away."

Jesus' wilderness experience had prepared Him for such a time. He was ready for success, and He wasn't tempted by it. This wasn't the kind of success He came to achieve. The people wanted to lift Him up and crown Him King in the manner they had crowned kings throughout the history of their nation.

Instead, Jesus chose downward mobility. He chose to identify Himself with every sinful man, woman, and child. His power was channeled in a most unique fashion by His choosing to come in the form of a suffering servant. He knew the cross wasn't far away. Instead of fighting it, strangely, He embraced it.

Paul wrote to the Philippians:

Do nothing out of selfish ambition or vain conceit, but in humility consider others better than yourselves. Each of you should look not only to your own interests, but also to the interests of others. Your attitude should be the same as that of Christ Jesus: Who, being in very nature God, did not consider equality with God something to be grasped, but made himself nothing, taking the very nature of a servant, being made in human likeness. And being found in appearance as a man, he humbled himself and became obedient to death—even death on a cross! (Phil. 2:3-8)

Of this passage Nouwen writes: "Here we touch the most important quality of Christian leadership in the future. It is not a leadership of power and control, but a leadership of powerlessness and humility in which the suffering servant of God, Jesus Christ, is made manifest" (Nouwen, p. 63).

This is the kind of downward mobility that we must contemplate. As you contemplate it during this Lenten season, ask yourself this question, "Was Jesus successful in changing the world?" If your answer is "yes," then I ask you, "Will you follow Him?"

Prayer

We can easily get lost in this wilderness, God. We are misled by worldly standards of success telling us that money, recognition, and power are the only ways out of the desert.

Humiliate us, Jesus. Hold our faults up to us as a mirror so we can finally see the absurdity of our sin. Take us to places where we can be honest with ourselves and honest with You. Call us out from hiding behind our secret shame; call us out in the nakedness of truth.

Humble us, Jesus. Redirect our hearts to follow Your ways. Bend our longings toward Your kingdom. Help us lift up the lowly and place ourselves in their seats. Bless us with a suffering servanthood that reminds us daily of Your mission.

Amen.

There's a Story with Every Scar
Lent 35

The scars my son carries on his right arm are ugly reminders of the day he was viciously attacked by a dog at my grandfather's house. If I stop and think of his screams for help for very long, they bring tears to my eyes. The scars tell the story of the horrific day when he was tossed around like a rag doll by a dog gone mad.

I have a scar just under my hairline on my forehead. Our family doctor removed an embarrassing birthmark when I was seventeen. The scar tells the story of why I kept my hair long as a teenager.

Chances are you have a scar somewhere, too, and every scar tells a story. Of course some scars can't be seen at all. They are buried in our psyche and in our memories, and yet, even they have a story to tell.

As Christians, when we die, we will shed this body like a cicada. The Apostle Paul, a tent maker by trade, likened living in this body to living in a tent, which we will one day lay aside (2 Peter 1:13). To the Corinthians, Paul said that the body is sown a natural body, but "it is raised a spiritual body" (1 Corinthians 15:44).

Everything that reminds us about our painful past will be gone when our body is raised "imperishable." All of our scars will be smoothed away. The physical scars from accidents and surgeries and attempted suicides will all be gone. The emotional scars from failures, disappointments, abuse, attacks, and lack of love will all be gone. The psychological scars from war, drug abuse, and child abuse will be gone.

So it's striking when Jesus appeared to His disciples in His resurrected body, a body like the one we can expect to have in heaven, free of decay, free of pain, free of suffering, that His body was NOT free of scars. The scars from the cross were still visible. Why didn't God fix Him up? Why didn't God smooth out those scars?

You cannot tell the story of Jesus without mentioning the scars He embodied. If you remove the scars of Jesus, you remove part of who He was and part of the reason He came to this earth. Erasing those scars would be like erasing part of the reason Jesus came to live among us.

Most of us want to leave our scars behind. Anything that reminds us of bad days, pain and suffering, of trucking through the wilderness, we want to leave behind in this world. We don't have any reason to believe we can't leave all of those scars here. But Jesus carried His scars into heaven with Him and that is intriguing.

We need a Jesus in heaven who still understands what our wounds feel like. The writer of Hebrews put it this way: "For we do not have a high priest who is unable to sympathize with our weaknesses, but we have one who has been tempted in every way, just as we are—yet was without sin" (Heb 4:15). Someone has said that the only things man-made in heaven are the scars of Jesus.

When Jesus first appeared to His disciples after the resurrection, they were locked in a room together, fearful that they might also receive the same fate as Jesus. Jesus suddenly appeared to them; He said, "Peace be with you!" (John 20:19). Then He showed them His hands and His side.

With a touch of irony, the same cross that had scattered the disciples just a few days earlier now brought the disciples peace. By showing them His scars, Jesus proved to the disciples that there was nothing He could not overcome, not even death.

Peace is possible when we have the one on our side who cannot be defeated, even by death. Jesus' scars brought the disciples peace and joy. I wonder if any of them recalled Isaiah 53:5: "The punishment that brought us peace was upon him, and by his wounds we are healed."

The scars of Jesus let the disciples know that the healing power Jesus exhibited in their ministry had only been interrupted by death, not destroyed. Because of His scars, the disciples knew their wounds, both physical and emotional, could be laid at His feet. He died to bring healing to us all.

By displaying His scars, Jesus reminded His disciples that He had found His way through the wilderness of death, the ultimate enemy, and peace through Him was possible.

The scars of Jesus helped the disciples begin to live their lives so that fear gave way to courage. Courage became possible because Jesus empowered them with the gift of the Holy Spirit. The disciples needed courage. At that moment they had no courage. They had only fear. When they saw the scars of Jesus and received the Lord's Holy Spirit, they knew that even if man should take their life for preaching the gospel of Christ, or even if man should inflict wounds upon their bodies that would leave permanent scars, in the end, God would work it all out to His good conclusion. They had seen the resurrected Lord, and they had seen His nail-scarred hands.

If we are into a life of self-preservation, as the disciples were when they locked themselves inside and closed out the world, what effect can we have on the world? Had they not been willing to subject themselves to their own set of scars for the gospel's sake, how would the world have been turned upside down for the sake of Christ?

Through the power of the Holy Spirit, which Jesus breathed upon them, it became possible for these people who were initially overcome by fear to have the power to overcome the world.

Thomas, who wasn't present when Jesus first met with the disciples after the resurrection, missed out on the initial blessing. Isn't it ironic that he said to the other disciples, "Unless I see the nail marks in his hands and put my finger where the nails were, and put my hand into his side, I will not believe it" (John 20:25)?

Thomas was a doubter, but he was closer to the Lord than he realized. Jesus had voluntarily presented His scars to the disciples when He met with them. These scars were reminders of His sacrifice. Jesus knew that the scars had power to cause others to believe.

Unlike before, when the disciples believed that Jesus would be a Messiah like King David, now they believed He was to be a Messiah as described in Isaiah: a suffering Messiah, a wounded Messiah, a justifying Messiah, an oppressed and afflicted Messiah, a dying Messiah, a Messiah who bore the sins of the world, a resurrected Messiah, a Messiah who healed others by His wounds and convinced others by His scars, and empowered others by the breath of His Holy Spirit.

In the end, it was Jesus' scars that made Thomas a believer, too. Jesus said to Thomas, "Put your finger here; see my hands. Reach out your hand and put it into my side. Stop doubting and believe." Thomas said to him, "My Lord and my God!" (John 20:27-28).

The scars of Jesus were enough to settle the issue for the disciples. Are those scars enough to settle the issue for you?

Prayer

Wounded Messiah, Your hands, Your feet, and Your side are an eternal testimony.

Your scars tell our story. It is a story of human sin, of betrayal and violence. It is a story that is hard for us to hear, so please pardon us when we turn away from You in our shame.

Your scars tell Your story. It is a story of Your sacrifice, Your love, and Your grace. It is a story we often forget when we get lost in the wilderness of our lives. Please help us hold this story deep within our hearts that we may accept Your good gifts.

Your scars tell God's story. It is a story of redemption and victory. It is a story that we sometimes cannot believe because it seems too good to be true, so please increase our faith when we doubt the divine promise.

May Your scars forever remind us of where we have been and where You are taking us.

Amen.

Who Is Willing
to Pick Up a Towel?
Lent 36

Walk for a few moments with Jesus and His disciples along the streets of Jerusalem. It's the week of the Passover, so the city has swelled with tourists, pilgrims, celebrants, and local citizens. They've gathered in the holy city for the greatest religious feast of the year.

Passover was the time when all faithful Jews celebrated the deliverance of the Israelites from Egyptian bondage. More than any other feast, Passover set the Jews apart as a people.

God's deeds of the past are very much on the minds of the people as they scurry about the town, but these are not the thoughts of Jesus' disciples. Their minds are on the future. The kingdom of God is near; it is about to burst in on them. Their Master has told them so. How can one think of feasts when something as important as this is about to take place? Their interest is in the kingdom, and, more importantly, their place in the kingdom.

We know some of the disciples had argued prior to this occasion about who among them was the greatest. Serving each other had given way to egotistical, self-serving thoughts.

As they make their way to the Upper Room where Jesus has had a meal prepared, I picture these disciples pushing and shoving like school children to vie for a seat closer to Jesus. Their patience with each other gets mighty thin. They are tired, and as they move on down, they shuffle their feet, raising clouds of dust, which cover their feet with an extra coating of dirt.

Jesus knows His disciples. He sees what is happening. He sees how their behavior has disintegrated and how their attitude is far from the humble, serving type of disciples He wants them to be. Time is running out for Him to teach them these things.

Finally the group makes its way to a small inn where the Master has made plans for their Passover meal, not just any meal, but a going-away party given by the One who should have been the guest of honor, a parting gift to the men Jesus loves so much.

However, no one feels much like having a party. Their bickering and jockeying for position have spoiled the mood and ruined the occasion. This is no time for His final teachings. None of them can hear Him. They are too busy thinking about their own positions in the kingdom.

It is a sullen, quiet group that climbs the stairs to that little room on the second floor where the simple meal has been laid out. Without saying a single word, they all decide to depart from their usual routine of one of them washing the feet of the others.

You've been there before, haven't you? Your attitude is in the gutter, so you don't pray before a meal. You don't open the door for a lady. You don't say "thank you" when extended kindness from another. You don't acknowledge God when you rise in the morning or before you close your eyes at night. You walk into a sanctuary, but you don't really expect to meet God or care if you meet anyone else.

You might ask, "Well, isn't it enough that I am here? Doesn't that make me better than those who chose not to come?"

As the men filed into the room, it was customary for one of the disciples to go over and pick up the basin of water and the towel, kneel in front of the others, and wash the sweat and grime of the road off the feet of his companions. Usually the lot fell to whoever was the first in the room. They had no servants to do it for them, so they voluntarily did it for one another.

But they were too preoccupied with their position in the kingdom to think about serving each other. If one of them stooped to perform this minimal task, it would be to admit to the others that he meant less to the kingdom.

So the meal starts with the dust of the road still on the disciples' feet, and Jesus is sick, sick in His heart because these are the men whom He loves and trusts and needs to carry on the work after He is gone. He sees their shortcomings, their human frailties, but all they can see is how faithful they have been to Him.

They feel they already have everything they need for the days ahead, but Jesus knows they have to be made to see how wrong they are. They have to be made to see what He has been telling them all along—that the first places in the kingdom are reserved not for those who are served, but for those who serve; otherwise, the future will become a wasteland. All Jesus has been teaching them will be for naught.

They have to be made to see that not one of them is perfect, that each still needs the Master's cleansing. So the Master Teacher, who has used parables to their fullest advantage all during His ministry, decides to act out a parable with a twofold message of renewal and self-sacrificial service.

In the middle of supper He rises from His place and lays aside His robe, just as He is later to lay aside His life for mankind, kneels down beside the men who all along have called Him teacher, and begins to wash the filth from their feet.

The room is silent. The tension is thick. As Jesus demonstrates His willingness to serve them, the men realize how petty, how selfish they have been. The water in the basin just gets dirtier and dirtier, and the men are made humbler and humbler with each pair of washed feet.

When He comes to Peter, the one who always has something to say, Peter protests Jesus' actions: "'No, you shall never wash my feet.' Jesus answered, 'Unless I wash you, you have no part with me'" (John 13:8-9).

Part of the Church's problem is that we show up without surrendering, and we wonder why we continue to wander in a wilderness. We are dictating to Jesus what portions of our lives He can touch and what portions are off limits. We think as long as we show up to a few worship services and attend a few meetings, God is somehow supposed to be pleased with us.

Jesus said, "Unless I wash you, you have no part with me." Put another way, "Unless you submit yourself to me and allow me to serve you, then you will have no part with me." Think about that—the Lord God wants to serve us!

Jesus' purpose on this earth was service. Through modeling service to us, He in turn wants service to become the centerpiece of our lives as well. We are supposed to be a reflection of our Lord.

We can talk it, we can preach it, we can become educated about it, but until we become a servant to others, we cannot fulfill God's purpose for our lives. When we are content to let others serve us and take no steps to serve others, we have not learned from the example of Christ. Our job as Christians is to help those in the wilderness find their way to a Promised Land.

Albert Schweitzer said that only those who learn to serve are happy. We serve by caring and helping to meet human needs, most especially the need everyone has for a relationship with God.[43]

Missionary Parkes Marler served in South Korea working among 550 lepers. When he first went to this assignment, he was afraid of these diseased people. Many had lost their fingers, hands, ears, and noses. They were all disfigured by the leprosy. However, he soon came to love them dearly. As he preached to them, a number became believers and were baptized.[44]

He told about hearing a Korean leper lady sing the gospel song, "Where He Leads Me I Will Follow." Because part of her lips were gone, the words sounded as if she were singing, "Where He Needs Me I Will Follow." That is the Christian's role and calling (White). Will we follow wherever Jesus needs us?

The great lesson of leadership from the military is that the troops will put up with a difficult life, often with intolerable conditions, if their leaders do the same. History is full of examples of the impact of the commander's presence on the front lines. It is said that General Lee made it a practice to visit the campsites of his troops the night before each major battle. Often he would do this at the expense of getting little or no sleep himself.

General Patton was often seen riding the lead tank of his armor units. His daring and courage were an inspiration to his men.

The Duke of Wellington, who defeated Napoleon at Waterloo, believed that Napoleon's presence on the battlefield was worth 40,000 soldiers.[45]

Now, who among us is willing to pick up a towel? It is the way of our Savior. It might have been the most important lesson Jesus taught to His disciples during the Passover week. During Lent, if we look around, we will find plenty of people with dirty feet. Some might be like Peter and will resist your efforts to serve them. Others will be humbled. Certainly all will see Jesus in you.

Prayer

God our Servant,

How many of us would stoop so low to wash another's dirty feet?

We confess we have been deceiving ourselves, believing that all it takes is a profession of a few words to become Your followers. Lord, help us understand that faith is action, that belief is doing, that we must move our feet in the wilderness to follow You. We need to be servants to one another, to live out our faith in humility like Jesus. Please allow our hearts and our hands to follow Christ's example, now and forevermore.

Amen.

Was Jesus Killed by a Rumor?

Lent 37

In January of 1987, two Southern California couples sat down to a modest meal of canned Menudo. Their meal had only begun when one of them discovered what looked like a human finger. Appetites apparently ruined, the shocked group carried the "finger" to a nearby hospital for testing.[46]

After leaving the hospital, they turned the "finger" over to an officer with the Azusa police department and told him that the object had been confirmed by a pathologist at Glendora Community Hospital as a human finger (Waters).

The police turned the "finger" over to federal food inspectors and gave a statement to the local newspaper. The story was picked up by UPI which also received a statement from the officer who had seen the "finger." He verified that it looked like a finger to him. "Radio commentator Paul Harvey told his audience—erroneously—that Juanita's products had been pulled from all Southern California grocery shelves. Harvey later ran a correction" (Waters). Why? Because the object wasn't a finger. No pathologist ever identified it as a finger, only a hospital employee who said it looked like one (Waters).

After testing, the "finger" was revealed to be was a piece of connective tissue commonly found in beef tripe, the main ingredient in Menudo (Waters).

The maker of Menudo, Juanita's Foods, hired a public relations firm to manage the fallout and committed $50,000 of its budget to high-profile damage control. But by then, it was too late. The rumor had already done its damage. Within four months of the rumor, sales had declined $1 million (Waters).

Other companies like Procter & Gamble have been victimized by some false rumors tying them to Satanism. This rumor was spread mostly by Christians convinced that the emblem on Procter and Gamble products was Satanic. Rumors swirled that the company gave a portion of its profit to support the Satanic church.

Do you remember Richard Jewell? Jewell was the security guard who spotted the green knapsack in Centennial Park minutes before it exploded during the 1996 Olympics in Atlanta. He alerted police and helped move people out of the area before the bomb exploded. One person was killed, and more than a hundred were injured. It could have been much worse had it not been for Jewell.

Because Jewell seemed to crave the spotlight, some investigators became suspicious. Three days after the bombing, the headlines of an *Atlanta Journal-Constitution* article read, "FBI Suspects Hero Guard May Have Planted Bomb." Rumors swirled around Jewell, rumors that proved to be false. For Jewell, it was too late. The damage to his reputation had already been done.

We live in a day when it's hard to separate factual news from rumors. Rumors are like poison darts. When they hit their target, they can have deadly results. Rumors have even been known to kill.

In January of 1692, a physician gave the unusual diagnosis of bewitchment to two girls who were displaying strange behavior. The diagnosis sent panic through the Massachusetts Bay Colony. Soon, rumors were coming from other parts of the village suggesting that there were others involved in witchcraft. This led to the infamous Salem Witch Trials. The rumors sent many to jail and, eventually, nineteen men and women to the gallows. Seventeen others died in prison. The story testifies to the danger of a rumor.

Did the same thing happen to Jesus? Was His life taken because of a rumor? Such a case can be made. When Jesus was crucified, His crime was written above Him on the cross: "THIS IS THE KING OF THE JEWS" (Luke 23:38). This charge was both truth and rumor. How could it be both?

When Jesus stood before Pilate, Pilate asked Him, "Are you the king of the Jews?" Jesus answered, "Is that your own idea...or did others talk to you about me?" (John 18:33-34).

Jesus was aware that people had called Him a king. In fact, they had welcomed Him as a king just days before His arrest when He came riding into Jerusalem on the foal of a donkey. But Jesus was not the kind of king that most people rumored Him to be. They were looking for a king who would sit on an earthly throne and rule the people and conquer other nations. For this very reason, Jesus never referred to Himself as the King of the Jews. He always used a more generic term, "Son of Man," when referring to Himself.

Jesus did not want to feed the rumor that He was to be a king like King David. He often told those who knew of His Messianic nature not to tell anyone because He knew that people would not be able to comprehend the truth about His kingdom at that time. Jesus clearly set the record straight with Pilate: "My kingdom is not of this world. If it were, my servants would fight to prevent my arrest by the Jews. But now my kingdom is from another place" (John 18:36).

Jesus wanted Pilate to know the truth. Jesus once referred to Himself as "the truth." He didn't want people following Him under false pretenses. He didn't want to feed the rumor mill. Rumors don't set people free. Rumors bind. Rumors destroy. Rumors pierce our souls. Rumors, once begun, spread like a California wildfire or a computer virus. Rumors injure. Rumors even kill.

> "'You are a king, then!' said Pilate. Jesus answered, 'You are right in saying I am a king. In fact, for this reason I was born, and for this I came into the world, to testify to the truth. Everyone on the side of truth listens to me.' 'What is truth?' Pilate asked" (John 18:37-38a).

The passage continues:

> With this he went out again to the Jews and said, "I find no basis for a charge against him. But it is your custom for me to release to you one prisoner at the time of the Passover. Do you want me to release "the king of the Jews"? They shouted back, "No, not him! Give us Barabbas!" Now Barabbas had taken part in a rebellion. (John 18:38b-40)

But it was too late. The damage of the rumor had already taken hold with the people. These people could not discern truth from lies and facts from fiction. These people who demanded Jesus' death were like Pilate; they did not know truth from rumor.

The wise men had it right from the beginning. Jesus was a king, but He was not the king He was rumored to be. Pilate didn't know truth and neither did the people who wanted Jesus executed. They knew only rumor. They knew only half the truth.

Many people have spent long periods of time in a wilderness caused by the careless and sometimes malicious rumors of others. If you have ever been on the receiving end of a rumor, either one that was intentional or unintentional, you should want to guard your speech for you know the pain rumors can cause.

Rumors have hurt companies, stopped careers, and even led to people's deaths. If Christians know the truth and have been set free by the truth, then we should handle rumors as we would handle toxic waste. Otherwise, we will become like one of those in the crowd who demanded that Barabbas, a known murderer, be released, while we nail truth to a cross. We will become responsible for causing others to walk into the wilderness with a heavy burden.

Prayer

Lord of Truth,

There is nothing more tempting to us than gossip. There is something about sharing the tragedy, embarrassment or sin of another, even if we don't know for sure that it's true, that makes us feel more powerful and alive.

But the opposite is true, for each time we help strengthen rumors, we weaken our own integrity and damage the reputations and lives of others. Safeguard us from this type of violence, the violence that banishes others to the wilderness, the violence that put Christ on the cross. Let us speak only what is good, pure and true. Let our words be the words of Christ; those words that build up and not destroy. In His holy name we pray, Amen.

Live Life
Like You Are Dying
Lent 38

In 2004, Tim McGraw's song, "Live Like You Were Dying," won song of the year and single of the year at the Country Music Association awards. The song is about a man in his forties who discovers he has a short time to live. Instead of feeling sorry for himself, he goes out and has every kind of positive experience he can with whatever time he has left.

The power of the song comes as this man ironically discovers a joy in life he's never had, even though he knows his time is short. His piercing words are challenging: "Someday I hope you get the chance to live like you were dying."[47]

I don't know whether McGraw's song has the power to change lives, but it has a powerful message to those who live life as if they will never die. If we live as if we will never die, our lives need to be changed because chances are we are living for the temporal and not for the eternal.

Every day we exchange part of our lives for something. According to Ofcom's annual Communications Market Report, Americans now spend over seven hours a day using technology. Because we are becoming so good at multi-tasking, we are actually cramming much more time with our technological devices into these seven hours.[48] That means Americans spend 106 days a year on computers, watching television, sending text messages, and talking on our cell phones. Would we change the way we spend any of our time if we knew we were dying?

Would we change the way we live if we knew we were dying? Guess what—we're all dying. Every day we inch closer to the grave.

Someone reading this book may not live another year. Sooner or later, the obituary column will carry our names. I believe McGraw is on to something with his song. If we lived like we were dying, many of the things we view as important would become trivial. If we lived like we were dying, many of the things we never get around to doing would get done.

McGraw sings,

"I was finally the husband that most of the time I wasn't / and I became a friend a friend would like to have / and all of a sudden going fishin' / wasn't such an imposition / and I went three times that year I lost my Dad / Well, I finally read the good book / and I took a good long hard look / at what I'd do if I could do it all again" (McGraw).

Jesus once told a parable about a man who became rich as a farmer. One year his crop was so bountiful that he couldn't store all of his grain, so he tore down his barns and built bigger ones. Now he had life made, and he said to himself, "'Soul, you have many goods laid up for many years; take your ease; eat, drink, and be merry.' But God said to him, 'Fool! This night your soul will be required of you; then whose will those things be which you have provided?' So is he who lays up treasure for himself, and is not rich toward God" (Luke 12:19-21 NKJV).

The farmer lived his life as if he'd never die. That's a recipe for a wilderness, a wilderness the Bible describes as lasting forever.

If we lived like we were dying, we'd be less materialistic and more concerned about our fellow man. We'd be less selfish and more giving. We wouldn't take life for granted. Rather, we'd wake up with hearts thankful for the gift of a single day. We would be less busy and more likely to notice the beauty of a rose or be more willing to sit with older people and hold their hands and listen to them share whatever's on their minds. If we lived like we were dying, we would be more intentional about saying "I love you," and we'd try harder to settle our differences with our neighbor. If we lived like we were dying, we'd be less concerned about our earthly bank account and more concerned about storing treasures in heaven.

Here's a news flash! We are all dying! We just don't know how long we have left to live. Now, what will you do with the time you have left? Lent is a good season to contemplate your answer.

Prayer

What if these were our last days, Jesus?

Would we spend our days with the television?
Or sitting in traffic?
Or cleaning our homes?
Eating alone?

Would we waste the rest of our lives being angry at our families?
Or ignoring phone calls from friends?
Or yelling at children?
Or complaining about our neighbors?

Would we squander the precious hours with regret?
Longing for the past?
Contemplating our mistakes?
Cursing our misfortune?

What if we lived our last days as You lived Yours, Jesus?

We would spend our days with people.
Sitting beside the lonely,
Going into people's homes,
Eating with outcasts.

We would invest the rest of our lives
Being with our families,
Talking with friends,
Embracing children,
Sharing with our neighbors.

We would devote the precious hours with thanksgiving.
Embracing the present moment,
Forgiving others of their mistakes,
Cherishing our blessings from God.

Teach us to be better investors of our time, Jesus.
Help us to live as if this day were our last.

Amen.

A Voice of Hope from an Urban Wilderness

Lent 39

In 1971, Gavin Bryars, one of England's leading musicians and composers, agreed to help his friend Alan Powers with the audio aspects of a film Powers was making about street people. The filming took place in an area around London's Waterloo Station. Powers filmed various people living on the streets. Some were obviously drunk, some mentally disturbed, but a few were articulate and easy to talk with.[49]

As Bryars made his way through the audio and video footage, he became aware of a repeating sound that always accompanied the presence of one older man. At first, the sound seemed like muttered gibberish. But after removing the background street noise and cleaning up the audiotape, Bryars discovered the old man was in fact singing (Bryars).

The song he sang under his breath was a simple, repetitive tune that he quietly sang uninterrupted for hours on end. Like a film loop, the song's final line fed into its first line, starting the tune over and over again without ceasing: "Jesus' blood never failed me yet/ Never failed me yet/ Jesus' blood never failed me yet/ There's one thing I know/ For He loves me so..." (Bryars).

One day, while playing the tape as background to other work, Bryars left the door to his studio open while he ran downstairs to get a cup of coffee. When he returned several minutes later, he found a normally buzzing office environment eerily stilled. The old man's quiet, quivery voice had leaked out of the recording room and transformed the office floor (Bryars).

Under the spell of this stranger's voice, an office of busy professionals had grown hushed. Those who were still moving around walked slowly, almost reverently about the room. Many more had taken their seats and were sitting motionless at their desks, transfixed by the voice. More than a few were silently weeping, tears cascading undisturbed down their faces (Bryars).

Bryars was stunned. Although not a believer himself, Bryars could not help being confronted by the mysterious spiritual power of this unadorned voice. Sitting in the midst of an urban wilderness, this John-the-Baptist voice touched a lonely, aching place that lurks in the human heart, offering an unexpected message of faith and hope in the midst of the darkest, most blighted night (Bryars).

This old homeless man had a gift; it was the gift of hope, a hope that sustained him, a hope that he gave away to others, without even knowing. To many he was brushed off as a half-crazed, homeless man. That day in Bryars' office, many professionals gathered round to hear that voice and wondered where that homeless man found his gift of hope, whether it was real, and whether they could find it too.

Where is hope? Where do we find hope? We must find hope, or we are doomed to wander forever in a wilderness of despair. Where hope is no longer found, we almost always choose to change our course. We must find hope in marriage, or our marriage will be doomed to un-happiness and it will likely be headed for the divorce court. We find hope in our work. If not, we often become unproductive and miserable. We may quit, get fired, or look for other work. We find hope in church or we stop attending. We find hope in prayer or we quit praying. We find hope in our leisure or we stop playing. We find hope in our faith or we stop believing.

During the Second World War, the Japanese held thousands of American soldiers captive. Forced to exist under inhumane conditions, many of them died. Others, however, survived and eventually returned home. There was no reason to believe there was a difference in the stamina of these two groups of soldiers. As a whole, the survivors did have this in common: they confidently expected to be released someday.

Researchers tell us we can live about fifty or sixty days without food, ten or twelve days without water, a few minutes without air. However, humanity cannot exist without hope. Somehow, some way, there has to be hope. Life is a process of hope dying and hope being born.

Sometimes hope needs to die while other hopes need to be born. You and I need the wisdom to know the difference between the two.

We might even learn something about hope from a homeless man with a song on his lips: "Jesus' blood never failed me yet / Never failed me yet/Jesus' blood never failed me yet / There's one thing I know / For He loves me so..."

Bryars, the English composer, started yearning for the confidence and hope this old man's song celebrated. He began to face what it meant to feel homeless and alone even when he was sitting in the midst of family. Bryars vowed to respect the homeless person by creating a recording that would celebrate and accentuate his simple message.

In 1993, England's leading contemporary composer, along with Philip Glass, one of America's leading composers, created and produced a CD titled "Jesus' Blood Never Failed Me Yet."

What convinced these leading musicians/composers to create a musical framework to preserve this old man's song? Why did an office full of busy people find themselves reduced to tears at the sound of his voice? How did this tiny scrap of audiotape from the cutting room floor ever survive to live on for hundreds of thousands to hear?

It survived because hope is a gift. It survived because God comes to us in mysterious, unpredictable, and surprising ways. During Lent, hear the words of hope spoken to Jesus by the thief on the cross, "Jesus, remember me when you come into your kingdom" (Luke 23:42). Jesus responded with hope: "I tell you the truth, today you will be with me in paradise" (Luke 23:43).

As we move closer to Easter morning, imagine the hopelessness the women must have felt as they approached the tomb to anoint the body of Jesus with spices. But when they got there the stone was rolled away, and they did not find Jesus' body.

Luke continues:

Suddenly two men in clothes that gleamed like lightning
stood beside them. In their fright the women bowed down
with their faces to the ground, but the men said to them,
"Why do you look for the living among the dead? He is not
here; he has risen! Remember how he told you, while he

was still with you in Galilee: 'The Son of Man must be de-
livered into the hands of sinful men, be crucified and on
the third day be raised again.' Then they remembered his
words." (Luke 24:4b-8)

Where are you looking for Christ to come this year? Can you sing
with the homeless man, "Jesus' blood never failed me yet/ Never failed
me yet / Jesus' blood never failed me yet / There's one thing I know / For
He loves me so..."?

Many times, the Lenten and Easter seasons pass us by because
we are not looking; we are not listening. But you are taking the time
to read this, so I'm confident that you have your hands open for God to
bless you and your ears open for God to speak to you.

During Lent and this Easter that is upon us, I pray that God will
surprise you in some mysterious, unpredictable and surprising way. I
pray that you will find in Him the hope that will sustain you, the hope
of a homeless man who once sang on the streets of London. For we worship a God who came to us in the flesh, who Himself was homeless in the
beginning, having to be placed in a feeding trough in a stable at birth,
then carried into Egypt to escape Herod. At death He had to be laid in a
borrowed tomb. Then He was raised triumphant, and His resurrection
gives us hope and sustains us still today.

His blood has never failed us. If a homeless man on the streets
of London can sing about it and help us find our way in our wilderness,
what about you? Can't you sing about it and help others find their way
through theirs?

Prayer

Expected Savior,

We are in the middle of waiting for a miracle just like the Israelites in the wilderness, just like the exiles in Babylon, and just like the disciples on that dark day after Jesus' death. Some of us wait for family members to come home. Some wait for loved ones to forgive us. Some wait for the economy to turn around. Some wait to be understood. Some wait to understand. Some wait for our marriages to heal. Some wait for You to bless us with children. Some wait for our lives to change. Some wait for our lives to start. Some wait for the world to find peace. And we all wait for You to answer our deepest, most intimate prayers.

Lord, help us find redemption in our waiting. Give us Your promise of hope in Your unyielding grace. Make Your hope known to us through Your life, death and resurrection. Give us hope in our doubt. Give us hope in our anger. Give us hope in our despair. And give us enough hope to give to others who so desperately need it.

Hope Incarnate, surprise us with Your mysterious and unpredictable grace!

Amen.

Lost in Grief
on Saturday
Lent 40

When pastoring my first church, I received a call one day from a stranger who wanted to know whether pets go to heaven. Her cat had died and it was more important to her than most people. I thought about telling her I was fairly certain all dogs go to heaven because I saw a movie about that once but I wasn't so sure about cats. This lady was very serious; it was apparent she really needed some empathy, not sarcasm. Who knows? Maybe there are animals in heaven.

It's amazing how much we love our pets, and how much love our pets give us in return. As a boy, I had a German Shepherd that was my best friend. She could hear the school bus coming from a half mile away. She would run up the road to meet it, and then run beside the bus all the way to the mobile home where my family lived, just to welcome me home. I'm convinced that if we welcomed members of our family home each day with the same joy our pets show us, home would be a nicer place to live.

I'll never forget the day Lady got too close to the bus as she ran beside it. It knocked her into the ditch. I held back my tears until after I got off the bus. I thought she was dead. I ran into the trailer crying to my mother. We found her up the road, under Mr. Kelsey Hamm's porch, licking her wounds.

We had her as a pet until she was about eleven. When Lady died, I cried like that boy did in the movie, "Old Yeller." We wrapped her in a blanket, dug a hole on the property behind our house, and buried her. I don't know whether Lady's in heaven or not, but she's still in my heart.

When my younger son Ryan was about five years old, he

experienced the death of his pet hamster, Rocky. Ryan had grown quite fond of his hamster. He would take Rocky out of his cage and let him run around in his room. He enjoyed getting him out and showing him off to people who came for a visit. Unfortunately, Ryan did not take very good care of his furry little friend. It did not take a Sherlock Holmes to discover the cause of Rocky's death. There was no water in the water dispenser and no food in the food bowl. The poor little fellow either died of lack of water or starved to death.

One benefit of children having pets is that they learn important aspects of life such as responsibility, love, and even grief. A child learns that all creatures eventually die, and if they are not fed and given water, they die sooner. A child's grief in the loss of a pet is a dress rehearsal for the deeper grief that life will surely bring.

The day we buried Rocky was a sad day for Ryan. I dug a hole for the hamster in the shadow of the church steeple while Ryan held him gently in his hands. I was tempted to eulogize him, but Ryan did not seem to be in the mood for sarcasm. Besides, he really was sad and I would not have trampled on his grief.

When it came time to place him in the hole, Ryan pitched him in the hole with a bit of angry force. It was certainly not the gentle placement I had expected. It was really a bit comical, although I held back a hint of a smile.

Anger is a stage in the grief process, but I'd not seen it expressed in quite that manner. Ryan cried most of the afternoon. I tried to be a consoling father. I knew I could not take his pain away. I just held him and listened to him. That's usually the best care we can give those who are grieving, whether it's a child grieving over the loss of a pet, or someone who is experiencing the depths of grief in the loss of a loved one.

Ryan's next pet was a cat named Tiger. I still don't know whether cats go to heaven, but after I let the garage door down on Tiger, I am positive they have more than one life.

One life is all we get, just one. Oh, there was Lazarus. After he had been dead for three days, Jesus gave him a rare second chance at living. There was also the daughter of Jairus, the synagogue leader, whom Jesus raised from the dead. But both Lazarus and Jairus' daughter eventually died again. Then there's Jesus.

The disciples had seen examples of people brought back to life after death. In addition to this, Jesus told his disciples on more than one occasion that he would be raised to life. Matthew 16:21 says: "From that time on Jesus began to explain to his disciples that he must go to Jerusalem and suffer many things at the hands of the elders, the chief priests and the teachers of the law, and that he must be killed and on the third day be raised to life."

Yet after the crucifixion and after Jesus' body had been laid in a borrowed tomb, there is not one shred of evidence in the gospels that the disciples expected anything miraculous to happen on Sunday. On Saturday, they were lost in their grief. On Saturday, they huddled together in fear. On Saturday, their dreams for the kingdom were lost. On Saturday, they had nothing but blank stares for one another, questions, anger, confusion, and despair. They were lost. They did not know where to go. They did not know what step they should take next.

Many people have sat where the disciples sat on that Saturday. Everyone deals with grief in life. Some people can go decades, though, and never deal with significant loss. People learn to cope with the small losses that happen along the way. Even a child can learn to cope and overcome the loss of a pet. But grief like the disciples were experiencing is immobilizing and crippling.

It's easy for us to judge the disciples and say, "They should have expected Jesus to be raised from the dead." However, such a miracle was still as foreign to their world as it is to ours, even though they had seen Jesus perform that miracle on two occasions.

It's important to ponder the emotional state of the disciples the day before Easter. Today, there are legions of people who live in that emotional state, locked in grief, immobilized by fear, unable to make sense of the events that have happened around them. Some of these people are people of faith, people who have been around Jesus all their lives, who have listened to His promises, but now are unable to hear His voice because of the tragedy that has befallen them.

Can Easter come to these people? Can they ever receive their joy again? Will God send a messenger to them to announce any news that they will interpret as good? The great hope of the Gospel for these people and for all of us is that the grief of Saturday is followed by the new life of Sunday morning, new life that is transforming and freeing, new life that lifts burdens and gives purpose. It's not a new life that answers all questions, but it is a new life that promises that God is with us, within us, working to redeem us, and using us to redeem others.

Prayer

Where are You, God?
In the silence of this day,
In the darkness of this hour,
When words cannot console,
And no light can illumine our path?

Where are You, God?
When we are dangling from the ledge of Your promises,
When we struggle to hold on to faith,
When our cries to you resound in empty echoes,
As grief pulls us deeper into the pits of despair?

Where are You, God?
When there seems to be no tomorrow,
When there is only this everlasting moment of pain,
As the seconds dig their heels into the pulling of time,
And the hours have halted their purposeful march?

Where are You, God?
When life has lost its meaning,
And nothing is certain but death,
When reality looms over us like a shadow,
And sleep is our only escape?

Where are You, God?
Are You near?
Come to us.

Be with Your people.
Help us.

Then Came Sunday

Tonya Harding—remember her? She's the professional ice skater who tried to have her competitor Nancy Kerrigan injured so that she wouldn't have to compete against her at the Olympics. After her career was put on ice, she turned to a less elegant and more primitive sport—boxing.

I used to be a big boxing fan. As a child, I was captivated by Mohammed Ali—as much by his mouth and personality as by his shuffling feet and lightning-quick jabs. I enjoyed his good humor and his playfulness with Howard Cosell, who did as much to make Ali a superstar as any of his trainers.

I met Ali once. The year was 1987. I had just completed my seminary training in Louisville, Kentucky. Christmas was only a few weeks away and so was my first job as a full-time minister. Before leaving Louisville, I strolled leisurely down the mall looking for Christmas gifts. I saw a small group of people gathered around a bench in the center of the mall. As I got closer, I heard laughter. Then as a couple of the people turned to leave, I saw Ali sitting down signing autographs on Islamic leaflets. I was shocked.

For the longest time I just stood there, star struck. He spoke softly, slowly, with great effort. His hands shook uncontrollably from Parkinson's Disease. His autograph was barely readable.

At the 1996 Olympics, the entire world saw how much his disease had crippled the man who was once the greatest boxer in the world. But in 1987, people still expected to see the same strong man who had lost and won the World Heavyweight Championship more than any other person in history. It was a shock for me to see such a strong man struggle to write his own name.

Jesus' disciples must have had shock ten times that great when Jesus, a real heavyweight in the Jewish world, was arrested, beaten, and eventually crucified. Though John is the only disciple the Bible says witnessed the crucifixion, all of the disciples believed Jesus was the greatest—until that day; that terrible day when they realized He was a man. But was He just a man? A misguided man? They thought He was more, but the cross dashed those beliefs.

As Jesus lay in a tomb, they gathered behind locked doors in fear. They were still in shock that a man who demonstrated miraculous powers over nature, demons, disease, and even death, could have been knocked out of their lives so quickly.

But then came Sunday! Evil had already counted to ten—K.O.! But that's the day Jesus got up off the mat to reach for and claim His heavyweight crown: resurrection day! Jesus was crowned the greatest of all time!

In the first scene of the movie *Rocky*, you hear the sounds of boxing gloves making contact with another person's body. You hear the shuffling of feet and the groans of two men struggling against one another, but you see the face of Jesus holding up the elements of the Lord's Supper.

Only when the camera pans wide do you realize that the setting is an old church that's been converted into a boxing arena. The image of Christ holding the elements of the Lord's Supper while two men struggle against one another in the ring below is a powerful image of what has happened and continues to happen as we do battle against evil.

We are in a struggle. Like Tonya Harding, we feel all that's left to do is to fight because of lost dreams or because of sins of our past. Like Ali we sometimes fight to hold together a body that no longer responds to our commands as it once did. Fame doesn't keep the battle at bay, nor does money, power, or religion.

While we cannot avoid the struggle, we need to be reminded that the victory is not in doubt. That is the reason the image of Jesus holding the elements of the Lord's Supper—the bread and the wine, elements that represent His body that was broken for us and His blood that was shed for us—is such a powerful image. That image hung over a boxing ring may never have been in a more appropriate place. That image reminds us that Jesus went to the mat for us. He took evil's deadliest blow—death, but He was not defeated.

When He rose from the grave on Easter morning, Jesus did so with the promise that He will join us in our corner. Having overcome death, He has the power to help us overcome any wilderness issue we might have.

So, as long as we live on this earth, we will journey through pain, difficulty, and many wilderness experiences. Just like the scene in *Rocky*, there's a struggle going on around us even when we cannot see it, but the scripture says that "our struggle is not against flesh and blood, but against the rulers, against the authorities, against the powers of this dark world and against the spiritual forces of evil in the heavenly realms" (Ephesians 6:12).

The Good News is that as we struggle, the Power of the Resurrection wants to be in our corner and He's immune from Parkinson's disease.

Prayer

Christ Everlasting,

This day life wins!
This day justice is championed!
This day hope is restored!
This day love reigns!

You have overcome the wilderness
And defeated death, Jesus!
Praise You, Lord!

You have made a path for others to travel,
A path of mercy, truth and grace!
Praise You, Lord!

You have walked beside us on our journeys,
And Your promises have shown us a way through!
Praise You, Lord!

You have shined Your light in the darkness,
And hate is destroyed.
Praise You, Lord.

This day You win, Jesus!
Praise be to You who fight
For a broken and hurting people!

Amen.

Bricks for Ricks Foundation

Royalties from this book go to The Bricks for Ricks Liberian Housing Foundation, Inc. This foundation was established in October 2008. The vision for the foundation was born in Liberia after I witnessed the terrible shortage of sustainable housing following Liberia's 14-year civil war.

I spent nearly one month in post-war Liberia in 2006 on the campus of Ricks Institute. During that time, I made my way into the area where the United Nations had set up a refugee camp during the war. In 1995 I had seen that refugee camp, which had housed over 20,000 displaced people. In 2006, there were still over 1,000 people there who had not made their way back to their villages. Their homes were the worst places of habitation I'd ever seen. Many could last only one or two more rainy seasons before being reclaimed by the elements.

One night while sleeping in my comfortable room on the campus of the school, I was awakened by a huge thunderstorm. I had to roll in the glass windows to keep my room dry. I knew the people in displacement camp were getting wet. The water from the storm had to be coming into their homes. The people in the camps slept on dirt floors. A few were fortunate enough to have a mattress.

That night, as clear as any time in my life, God spoke to me. "You need to do something about those people in the camp who have no shelter from the storm."

In the story of Jesus feeding the five thousand, He asks the disciples where they can purchase food to feed the people, knowing that He was going to feed them Himself. He wanted the disciples to struggle with the answer to His question (Matthew 6:5-6).

I think that's what God wanted me to do that night, struggle with my comfortable room, with the knowledge that those people were getting wet, not only that night, but every night it rained. With the rainy season coming (about 170 inches fall in Liberia in six months), I could not imagine the kind of misery they lived with day in and day out.

What I experienced sixteen miles outside of Monrovia is repeated all over this earth. "The U.N. Human Settlements Program estimates that more than 1 billion rural dwellers and 600 million urban residents in developing countries live in overcrowded housing with poor water quality, lack of sanitation and no garbage collection."[50]

As the population of the world continues to increase, passing the seven billion mark in 2011, the pressure on the world's resources continues to increase as well. The truth is, sharing facts such as these typically doesn't move many people into action. The game changer for me happened that night during the storm.

You see, up until that time, I didn't know anyone in a Third World country who needed shelter. Now I see faces. Now I know names. I realize that these are people with hopes and dreams that are not unlike the ones you and I have. They want education for their children. They want to earn a wage. They want to worship in a church. They want a comfortable place to eat and sleep.

Less than a week after the storm, I attended a meeting at the Monrovia Rotary Club and met a retired hospital administrator who had moved to Liberia to build orphanages. He was using an earth block press to make blocks from a mixture of earth and a small portion of cement. That seemed to me to be God's way of saying, "Here's a way to take the earth, My own provision, and multiply it into the raw materials you need to help people build their homes, schools, and churches."

Two years later I began the Bricks for Ricks Foundation with that dream in mind and began a search for the best earth block machine I could find on the market.

In November of 2011, the Bricks for Ricks Foundation, in conjunction with First Baptist Church Jefferson, received the first BP-714 Earth Block Press produced by the Vermeer Corporation. This machine produces an interlocking block, designed by Adam de Jong (www.dwellearth.com). The machine is run by a Hatz diesel engine which powers a hydraulic compression chamber. Its two piston rams force the dirt to the edges of the block, giving each block a consistent PSI rating. The two center holes it creates allow reinforcing bar to be run through the block where needed and cement to be poured to make vertical cement columns at the corners, door facings and windows.

The machine has no electronics, no battery, starts with a hand crank, and has few moving parts, thus requiring little maintenance. It can produce four, twenty-pound blocks per minute. It uses 94% dirt and 6% Portland cement. These compressed blocks are really just a modernized version of the way earth blocks have been made for centuries. The difference and the "magic" is the small amount of Portland cement added to the dirt, along with the compression, which keeps the block from breaking down in the elements.

Soil is one of the most available and cheapest natural resources. It's also one of the best building materials and has been used for thousands of years. The oldest, continuously lived in earthen masonry building is in the Western Hemisphere in the Lima, Peru basin and is over 3,500 years old."[51]

Geological Surveys show that 65-70 percent of the soil present on the Earth's surface is a likely candidate for making compressed soil blocks (Fifth Wind)."

Not only is soil readily available and cheap, but as a building material it can be made stable. With its strength and with the ability to add vertical and horizontal reinforcements, buildings made with earth blocks can be built in seismic zones with confidence. Buildings made with earth block are bullet proof and bug proof. Compared to cinder block, compressed earth blocks (CEB's) are less than half the cost to make. They are stronger, (U.S. code for cinder block is 1900 PSI, compared to blocks of 2500 PSI that Dwell Earth tested with the BP-714), and buildings made with these blocks produce about a ten degrees difference of inside temperature.

I realize that in a world where hundreds of millions of people need sustainable shelter, my small foundation may not make much difference. However, in the beginning, Millard Fuller's dream with Habitat for Humanity started off small.

It's one thing to go to another county and build a house for those with inadequate or no housing at all. It's quite another to provide people with the skills and tools to build their own homes, schools, and churches. The Bricks for Ricks Foundation is committed to helping "the least of these" of the world help themselves by equipping them with the tools and the knowledge they need to construct their own dwellings.

God willing, machines will be shipped to Virginia, Liberia and Lima, Peru in 2012, followed by trained teams to teach soil excavation, machine usage, and block-laying techniques. We believe this is a new and exciting way for churches to do missions.

As we build homes, we also build community, something Joe Morgan, one of the deacon's at First Baptist Church Jefferson, noticed as people young and old gathered in the parking lot of our church to make our blocks.

You may never travel to some of the most impoverished parts of the world and see the living conditions of these people. If you did, many of you would be compelled to do something to help them like I am trying to do. However, you can travel there with our foundation. You can allow the Bricks for Ricks Foundation to help these people on your behalf.

Millard Fuller believed that every person ought to have a decent place to live. Since so many people don't, I'm hoping to make a difference for a few. If the royalties from this book lead to one family in Peru, Liberia, or anywhere else in the world to have a decent place to sleep, worship, or study, what a blessing that will be! However, I am hoping for a village.

Help us help the "least of these."

Make your checks payable to:
Bricks for Ricks Foundation

Mail checks to
Jefferson First Baptist Church
81 Institute Street
Jefferson, GA 30549

All donations will be acknowledged.

You may order other books by this author at www.johnmichaelhelms.com or at www.Amazon.com. Also look for these websites: www.bricksforricks.org and www.thefaithlab.com.

Scripture Reference Guide

Introduction
Matthew 28:6
Psalm 103:15-16

Lent 1
Revelation 20:14-15
Luke 23:42-43
James 4:14
Genesis 3:19
Mark 1:15

Lent 2
John 19:9-11
Hebrews 4:15-16

Lent 3
Psalm 121:5-6
Mark 4:30-32

Lent 4
Matthew 6:20
Psalm 23:6

Lent 5
Ecclesiastes 2:10-11

Lent 6
1 Samuel 9:2, 16:7b
1 Corinthians 13:12

Lent 8
Job 41:1-5, 10-11
Job 42:2-3

Psalm 74:12-14
Isaiah 27:1

Lent 9
Luke 19:5-7
Luke 19:8-10
1 Corinthians 13:5

Lent 10
Matthew 7:3
Romans 3:23
1 John 1:9-10

Lent 11
Mark 12:30
Matthew 19:22
Mark 12:43-44
Matthew 26:39
Matthew 16:24-26

Lent 12
Proverbs 18:24
Matthew 18:12

Lent 13
Acts 16:25, 31-34

Lent 14
Ezekiel 36:25-27

Lent 15
Romans 10:15

Lent 16
2 Samuel 11:1
1 Kings 9:4-5

Lent 17
Luke 17:17

Lent 18
Proverbs 14:12

Lent 19
Deuteronomy 10:18-19
1 Peter 4:9-10
Hebrews 13:2

Lent 20
Luke 23:47
Luke 6:30
Matthew 18:8-9
Acts 16:35-37

Lent 21
Numbers 11:4-6
Numbers 11:11-15

John 11:21-22

Lent 22
1 Samuel 9:2
1 Samuel 16:7
1 Corinthians 6:19-20
1 Corinthians 15:50

Lent 23
Ruth 1:19-21
Job 1:21
Ruth 4:14-16
Ephesians 4:31-32

Lent 24
Romans 12:3
Revelation 3:12

Lent 25
Philippians 2:7-8
Matthew 4:2-4
Luke 10:27
John 19:8-11
Matthew 26:50-53
Luke 23:34
John 19:30

Lent 26
John 11:21-27
John 14:1-3
Revelation 7:17
Matthew 13:49-50
John 11:4

Lent 27
2 Corinthians 7:4
2 Corinthians 11:23-29

Lent 28
1 Peter 5:6-7

Lent 29
Acts 10:35b
Proverbs 29:18
Luke 18:27

Lent 30
Exodus 33:12-17
Matthew 7:23

Lent 31
Deuteronomy 34:4b
Psalm 90:4-6, 10, 12
Numbers 20:12

Lent 32
Proverbs 22:1
Matthew 5:42

Lent 33
Matthew 16:16
Luke 22:44

Lent 34
Matthew 4:5-7
Matthew 21:9
Philippians 2:3-8

Lent 35
1 Peter 1:13
1 Corinthians 15:44
Hebrews 4:15
John 20:19
Isaiah 53:5
John 20:25, 27

Lent 36
John 13:8-9

Lent 37
Luke 23:38
Luke 18:33-40

Lent 38
Luke 12:19-21

Lent 39
Luke 23:42-43
Luke 24:4b-8

Lent 40
Matthew 16:21

Then Came Sunday
Ephesians 6:12

Bricks for Ricks
Matthew 6:5-6

Endnotes

[1] "Easter," *Wikipedia*, www.wikipedia.com, n.d., Hereafter cited in the text.

[2] "Lent 2011," *Campus Ministry, Georgetown University*, http://campusministry.georgetown.edu/88635.html.

[3] Dennis Bratcher, "The Season of Lent," *The Voice*, 2010, http://www.cresourcei.org/cylent.html. Hereafter cited in the text.

[4] All biblical references are to the NIV unless otherwise noted.

[5] Dan Graves, "Reformed Churches Muzzled but Protest at Barman," *Christianity.com*, May 2007, http://www.christianity.com/ChurchHistory/11630758/. Hereafter cited in the text.

[6] Mary Fairchild, "General Statistics and Facts of Christianity," *About.com*, 2011, http://christianity.about.com/od/denominations/p/christiantoday.htm.

[7] Eric Lemonholm, "Happy Father's Day 2006," *Lemonholm* (blog), June 18, 2006, http://lemonholm.blogspot.com/search?q=garden+when+God+had+it+by+himself.

[8] Tim O'Keefe, "Epicurus," *Internet Encyclopedia of Philosophy*, April 13, 2001, http://www.iep.utm.edu/epicur/.

[9] Alice Frying, *Seven Lies About Sex*, (Downers Grove, IL: Intervarsity Press, 1997).

[10] Quoted in "Letters to Malcolm 17: Pathways to Adoration," *The Pocket Scroll* (blog), May 7, 2010, http://mjjhoskin.wordpress.com/2010/05/07/letters-to-malcolm-17-pathways-to-adoration/.

[11] Barna Research Group, Ltd., "Americans Are Most Likely to Base Truth on Feelings," *Barna Group*, February 12, 2002, http://www.barna.org/barna-update/article/5-barna-update/67-americans-are-most-likely-to-base-truth-on-feelings.

[12] Leena Palande, "Plants in the Rainforest," *Buzzle.com*, March 13, 2010, http://www.buzzle.com/articles/plants-in-the-rainforest.html. Hereafter cited in the text.

[13] "Play/Pleasure/Relaxation," *MyCatholicSource.com*, 2001-2011, http://www.mycatholicsource.com/mcs/qt/catholic_activities_reflections.htm#Play / Pleasure / Relaxation.

[14] "Eyes and Vision," *Home Science Tool: The Gateway to Discovery*, 2011, http://www.hometrainingtools.com/eye-and-vision-science-explorations-newsletter/a/1255/. Hereafter cited in the text.

[15] Garth Kermerling, "Socrates: Philosophical Life," October 27, 2001, http://www.philosophypages.com/hy/2d.htm.

[16] Larry McShane, "Poker Boom is Picking Up a Much Younger Crowd," *Katu.com*, June 23, 2008, http://www.katu.com/entertainment/3626586.html.

[17] "True Friends Visit," Peace andSerenity, November 14, 2010, http://asianmountaincowboy.blogspot.com/2010/11/friends-visit.html.

[18] *Singing in the Rain*. Directed by Stanley Donen and Gene Kelly. 1952. Retrieved June 9, 2011 from http://www.youtube.com/watch?v=D1ZYhVpdXbQ.

[19] Arthur Freed, "Singing in the Rain," 1929, http://www.stlyrics.com/lyrics/singinintherain/singinintherain.htm.

[20] "Quotations that Focus on Perseverance," n.d., *Great Expectations*, http://www.greatexpectationsok.org/implementation_viewquotes.php?type=2#.

[21] Quoted in Richard Innes, "Integrity," *Acts International*, n.d., http://www.actsweb.org/test/articles/article.php?i=152&d=2&c=13.

[22] Jim Moore, "Go 2 Guy: Like Price, a heavy price," *Seattle PI*, May 6, 2003, http://www.seattlepi.com/moore/120854_moore07.html.

[23] Dick Innes, "A Simple 'Thank You' Will Suffice," *Acts International*, n.d.,http://www.actsweb.org/articles/article.php?i=207&d=1&c=2&p=1.

[24] Chris Smith, "A Simple Remedy for Depression," Church of Christ Smithville, TN, Online Church Bulletin, http://www.smithvillechurch.org/html/a_simple_remedy_for_depression.html. Hereafter cited in the text.

[25] Richard G. Wimer, "Special thoughts," *Wit and Wisdom*, March 25, 2005, http://www.witandwisdom.org/archive/20050325.htm.   Hereafter cited in the text.

[26] Jon Gambrele, "United Nations Marks 7 Billionth Baby," October, 31, 2011, http://news.yahoo.com/united-nations-marks-7-billionth-baby-194705498.html.

[27] Bill Versteeg, "Living Stones Theology: The Gift of Hospitality," *Online Sermons Page*, 2000, http://www.pbv.thunder-bay.on.ca/NetSermons/1pet4ser.html. Hereafter cited in the text.

[28] Sarah at Parenting, "True Mom Confessions," *Parenting.com* (blog), April 15, 2009, http://www.parenting.com/blogs/show-and-tell/true-mom-confessions.

[29] Deon Binneman, "Frogs make noise. Why don't we?" *WordPress* (blog), December 1, 2009, http://deonbinneman.wordpress.com/2009/12/01/frogs-make-noise-why-dont-we/.

[30] "Sermon Illustrations," Category: Conflict, *Preaching.com*, 2010, http://www.preaching.com/sermon-illustrations/11574760/.

[31] Outreach, Inc., Illustration results for "basketball." Category: Humor, *Sermoncentral.com*, 2010, http://www.sermoncentral.com/ illustrations/humorous-illustrations-about-basketball.asp.

[32] Thresiapaulose, "In the New Year, Use Skills, Not Pills to Kill Your Stress," *Healthmad*, December 28, 2010, http://healthmad.com/mental-health/in-the-new-year-use-skills-not-pills-to-kill-your-stress/.

[33] "Country Woman," ed. Ann Kaiser, November/December, 1990.

[34] Daniel Bagby, Shared comments by the author, with permission. Hereafter cited in the text.

[35] Adam Galinsky and Joe Magee, "Power Corrupts? Absolutely," *U.S. News and World Report*, January 29, 2007, http://www.usnews.com/usnews/ biztech/articles/070129/29power.htm. Hereafter cited in the text.

[36] Andrae Crouch., "Lyrics Mania," *Soon and Very Soon*, http://www. lyricsmania.com/soon_and_very_soon_lyrics_andrae_crouch.html.

[37] Randy Pausch, "The Last Lecture," http://www.youtube.com/watch?v =j7zzQpvoYcQ&feature=fvst.

[38] Viktor Frankl, *Man's Search for Meaning* (Boston: Beacon Press, 1984), p. 75.

[39] Bill Irwin, Blind Courage (Appalachian Trail Conference, 1997), p. 37.

[40] Robert E. Rivers, Jr., "HR 1367-Stroud, Cleveland; commend," March 18, 1998, http://www1.legis.ga.gov/legis/1997_98/fulltext/hr1367. htm. Hereafter cited in the text.

[41] Henri Nouwen, *The Wounded Healer* (New York: Doubleday, 1979) p. 77.

[42] Henri Nouwen, *In the Name of Jesus*, (New York: Crossroad, 1989), p. 10. Hereafter cited in the text.

[43] "Happiness Sayings," *Happyhalfway.com*, n.d., http://www.happy halfway.com/happiness-sayings.html.

[44] Harold L. White, "Will You Follow?" Sermon Storehouse, n.d., http:// wharold10.freeweb7.com/john13117.html. Hereafter cited in the text.

[45] John C. Maxwell, *Everyone Communicates: Few Connect* (Nashville: NavPress Publishing, 2010), p. 237.

[46] Tim Waters, "Firm Says Report of Finger in Soup Cost It $1 Million: Juanitas Foods' Claim Against Azusa Rejected," *Los Angeles Times*, May 7, 1987, http://articles.latimes.com/1987-05-05/news/cb-4456_1_azusu-police-department. Hereafter cited in the text.

[47] Tim McGraw, "Live Like You Were Dying," n.d., http://www.cowboylyrics.com/lyrics/mcgraw-tim/live-like-you-were-dying-13619.html. Hereafter cited in the text.

[48] Liz Thomas and Paul Revoir, "Computers and TV take up half our lives as we spend seven hours a day using technology," *Mail Online*, August 19, 2010, http://www.dailymail.co.uk/news/article-1304266/We-spend-7-hours-day-using-technology-computers-TV-lives.html.

[49] Gavin Bryars, "Jesus Blood Never Failed Me Yet," http://www.gavinbryars.com/Pages/jesus_blood_never_failed_m.html.   Hereafter cited in the text.

[50] Partners in Health, "Food, Water, and Housing," 2009-2010, http://www.pih.org/pages/food-water-and-housing/.

[51] Fifth Wind, "Making Compressed Earth Blocks," http://fifthwindfarm.blogspot.com/p/making-earth-blocks.htm.

CPSIA information can be obtained at www.ICGtesting.com
Printed in the USA
LVOW070301310112

266293LV00002B/2/P